How I Gained My Vision By Losing It

by Charles Lee Sidi

How I Gained My Vision By Losing It

by Charles Lee Sidi

Editor Aashay Sanghvi

Foreword by Rabbi Pinchas Allouche

Sidi Publishing 2014

First Printing: 2014

ISBN: 1503192660
ISBN 13: 9781503192669
Library of Congress Control Number: 2014920323
CreateSpace Independent Publishing Platform
North Charleston, South Carolina

For my wife, Sarah,

I am Nay above you, I am Nay below you
I am always by your side.

Contents

Acknowledgements

Thank you to my editor Aashay, a young man with a great journey ahead of him. Thank you to my dear friend Pinchas for writing the foreword and for being a true inspiration to many.

To all the collaborators in my life, I sincerely thank you.

Foreword by Rabbi Pinchas Allouche

"If you lose your money, you've lost nothing.
Money comes and money goes.
If you lose your health, you've lost half.
You are not the person you were before.
But if you lose your resolve, you've lost it all."
- Hassidic Proverb.

The story you're about to read is about a dear friend, Charles, who has never lost his resolve. His life, as you will see, is filled with enthusiastic ups and dispiriting downs, staggering successes and disheartening failures, resounding victories and heartbreaking defeats. Yet amazingly, throughout his life's many twists and turns, Charles' resolve remains robust and strong.

With brutal honesty and unashamed candidness, Charles takes us, the readers, into the chambers of his inner, transparent self. His eloquent words are personal yet personable, private yet inviting, intimate yet engaging. And his life, as you will discover, is nothing short of inspiring.

Yet, as we embark on Charles' many journeys, many readers may wonder: is his story real? How can that be? How can a person who has lost his vision, see again? How can an entrepreneur who has tumbled, rise again? How can an intelligent being who's been defied by logic so many times, believe again?

The reason, I believe, is rooted in Charles's vision of life. To paraphrase John F. Kennedy: "When written in Chinese, the word 'crisis' is composed of two characters. One represents danger and the other represents opportunity." Kennedy's message was poignant. Indeed, when presented with a crisis, many choose to focus on its dangers.

But Charles's vision, as evident in this book, is different. When faced with a crisis, Charles always searches for the opportunity within, with unwavering resolve and indefatigable conviction. And with such a penetrating vision, Charles demonstrates to us all, that no challenge can ever be too big, no obstacle can ever be too tall.

As I read the concluding chapter of this book, a line from a song by Leonard Cohen, popped in my mind: "Forget your perfect offering," Cohen suggests. "There is a crack in everything. That's how the light gets in." Thank you, Charles, for the gift of this book, and for sharing with us your vision that continues to melt away your 'cracks', and ours.

May God bless you, Charles, with continued health, strength and joy, to continue to serve as a beacon of light, to all who come in contact with you, with your words, and with your vision. Amen.

Introduction by Aashay Sanghvi

I wake up every morning and ask myself, "What's the next big idea that's going to make a big impact in this world?" I continue to ask myself this very important question every day because I, clearly, have not found the answer yet. This is very important for me this year. I am eighteen years old, and on my gap year before I start school at Harvard in 2015. I have a lot of time this year to explore and reflect. But, I'm not alone in this journey. I have many mentors that are willing to help me and prod me along in my life. I believe it is the mentorship that keeps me going and prevents me from getting frustrated. I believe that every person needs some form of mentorship in his or her life. Mentors allow one to push his or her boundaries, yet stay grounded at the same time. They are both the encouragers and the naysayers of one's ideas.

In my life, I am blessed and fortunate to have many mentors. However, there is one man who sticks out. I've only become very close with Charles Sidi recently, but I have been great friends with his oldest son, Adam, for a few years now. As friends, Adam and I share similar interests and thought processes about life. Even though he is much older than I, Charles and I also tend to think the same way. He is a great friend, role model, and mentor in my life. I aspire to be as creative, passionate, and entrepreneurial as he is one day. When he asked me to edit his book during my year off, I jumped at the opportunity. Not only do I have the extra time during my sabbatical, I also had the excitement.

Yet, Charles has had his demons. Who among us has not? He has been courageous enough to share his struggles and the insight into life that followed after. As I think about this book, I am reminded of a painting by the French artist Paul Gauguin. In Tahiti, Gauguin painted a masterpiece entitled, "Where Do We Come From? Who Are We? Where are we going?" Although this book is about the journey Charles took to save his vision, it is also about these questions that plague our existence on this planet. I couldn't be prouder to have been part of this process, and I can't wait to see what the future holds. Charles has chosen to make his life a work of art, and he is the artist.

Chapter 1: I Can't See

"**S**orry Charles, but it's not good news."

Shit! I've heard this before, I thought. I look at my wife Sarah, who is trying to be brave, but is clearly distressed. My whole body is descending into the ophthalmologist's chair as I try to comprehend what I have just heard. I feel completely suspended in motion as my life flashes before me. My worst nightmare is coming true.

"Is there nothing you can do?" I ask the tired-looking doctor who has kindly come to his office to see me after a night out with his friends. It is now just after midnight, and the doctor's office is so quiet and peaceful, which feels strangely pleasant. It is funny how an environment can seem so different without its usual occupants. At least I don't have to wait in line!

"Can't you laser it back in place?" I ask frantically.

The doctor is kind and gentle with me, and he seems genuinely concerned. I had already been to his office that week—twice actually—to see one of his colleagues and this visit was not expected at all. He leans back in his chair while removing his glasses to rub his nose.

"No, you're going to need surgery right away," he says, quite regrettably. Panic sets in pretty quickly, and I feel my stomach flip over and over while my head is spinning. Here I am, on vacation in

San Diego, California, with my wife Sarah and my two boys Adam and Joshua. Hundreds of miles from my home in Phoenix, Arizona. So many questions are now going through my mind all at once. The words *fuck*, *shit*, and *wanker* as well.

The kind doctor is now talking to me, describing all my options, and I can see his lips moving, but the words are not registering. It is like a silent movie without the subtitles. I am completely zoned out. The room is dimly lit except for the light beaming from the doctor's head-light contraption that he has just blinded me with while doing his examination. As the initial blindness from his head-light starts to fade, I notice my poor wife sitting in a chair in the corner of the room, a tear is glistening down her soft face. She knows what is coming and so do I. You see, this is not the first time an eye doctor has told me I need surgery right away. This is actually the second time, but this time, it's different. The retina has detached in my only good eye.

Fuck, shit, wanker—pops into my mind yet again. I'm screwed—I could go blind. I put on a brave face and blurt out,

"Right! Let's get back to Phoenix and see my doctor there and get him to do the surgery." The doctor and my wife are in deep conversation as I interrupt them. We toss around the idea of that for a while, going back and forth about whether I should stay in San Diego and have the surgery or go home to Phoenix. I am now singing in my head the famous Clash tune, "Should I Stay or Should I Go?" You know the one.

"Charles, Charles! I agree let's get back to Phoenix; I'll drive," Sarah says and interrupts the song in my head. She sees that I am in a daze so she takes control of the situation. She knows the drill and goes into overdrive. Everything is blank, and it feels like I am walking in mud. My legs are heavy, and I'm visibly shaking.

We head off into the dark night after thanking the doctor for coming out and how truly sorry we are for ruining his evening. Being British, we still somehow manage to say sorry, even though the world is falling apart around us. It's in our DNA I guess. As we leave the doctor says,

"Charles, make sure you lie on your right hand side all the way home otherwise the retina could further detach and cause permanent blindness." *Bloody brilliant!*

Chapter 2: It's A Long Journey

What should only be a twenty-minute drive back to the apartment on Coronado Island seems to take forever. The car is quiet except for the sound of the wheels running against the black top as I lie on my right hand side with my head looking out the window. I can see the overhead lights flash on and off as we speed down the freeway. All I can think about is how am I going to get through this. Sarah is now talking to herself about how she can get the apartment packed up in thirty minutes and that we should be able to drop the boys off with my business partner, Rick.

"Hopefully, they can stay with Rick and Liz," she says calmly, "I really don't want them to have to go through all this again." I just nodded in agreement, knowing I will soon have to wake up my two boys Adam and Joshua to tell them that the retina in my right eye has detached and that we will have to get back to Phoenix in order to be there by the morning. I check my watch and, I see that it is now after 1:00 AM.

There is something very weird about a detached retina because there is actually no pain, and you can still see as if nothing is wrong. However, you can feel the retina moving around as you move your eye, which is rather strange. The important thing now is that I have to get it surgically fixed within the next twenty-four hours or the chance of saving my eye will get slimmer as the days go by. I learned this harsh lesson with my left eye five years earlier. Unfortunately, thanks to the incompetence of a "doctor," I went without surgery for three months and it never really recovered, which left me with no macular vision. This essentially means I can't see any detail out of the eye. I know that this time around, detaching my only good eye would leave me with very little sight.

I call my business partner and good friend Rick. Rick is a great guy with a big heart, so I know he would be okay to look after the boys for a few days. I am not sure how he will feel about his partner being out of action for quite some time, possibly left with little to no vision, without the ability to create and invent new products. After all, it was I who had motivated him to become CEO of my start-up company BizBox two years earlier.

After what seems like a complete blur, I'm now standing in the parking garage with my two boys, Sarah, Rick, and his wife, Liz. Liz gathers us into a circle to say a prayer for our journey home and my ensuing surgery. My wife has indeed managed to pack up the apartment in thirty minutes and arrange everything while remaining stoic with black coffee in hand, ready for the long drive home through the night.

"Please take Charles and Sarah safely home to Phoenix and may the surgeon's hand be guided by you, Oh Lord," Liz says confidently and calmly. I'm just standing there dazed and thinking, Liz, I love you for this moment of peace and tranquility amongst all the chaos. We are all in tears and I look at my boys' faces, which are crumpled with emotion after being woken up in the dead of the night to find out their dad might lose his sight. When this happened last time, it was many months before I could see my boys' faces again properly. We say our goodbyes and as we drive off, I look in the side view mirror and see my boys' faces for what could be the last time. It is brutal watching them get smaller and smaller in the distance, and the thought of leaving them behind in this stressful situation only added to my despair.

Sarah takes control of the car with great confidence while sipping her coffee to keep her awake. I know that inside, she is panicking, but is doing everything she can to remain calm. It's now past 2:00AM, and I'm thinking it's at least a six-hour drive to Phoenix. I am helpless, apart from being able to talk to her to keep her alert as she navigates the windy roads into the desert. This situation is truly awful, but for some weird reason, I feel completely free and so does Sarah. I know the boys are safe with Rick and Liz and they would fly home in a few days after the surgery was over.

We are on the open road, driving through the night with nothing but each other, the car, and the desert. The stars look amazing in the dark sky, and the warm Californian air brings a sweet smell of nostalgia. It's like old times with Sarah and I, driving and talking, feeling as free as the time we traveled to London to see her father and tell him we had just become engaged.

"Do you remember that time when we drove to London to see your father?" I say to Sarah.

"Yes, my poor dad had never met you before and you walked in and said, 'Hi Graham, nice to meet you. I'm your new son-in-law!'" she says laughing.

"I know it was crazy, and we had only been together for seven weeks. He took it really well," I reply.

Sarah and I first met in the summer of 1994, at a local pub in our hometown, near Manchester, UK. As funny as it sounds, we weren't particularly attracted to one another initially. But I thought she was completely different from other girls I had dated. One example of this was our first date—we went for a run, yes, a run. I had and have always tried to stay fit and healthy, and Sarah was the kind of girl who was up for a laugh and agreed when I asked her out on this unusual date. I picked her up, and we went to the local park. I noticed her legs looked really tanned, but then I realized she had put tights on under her shorts. Just for a laugh, I said we needed to stretch our legs so we didn't pull a muscle or something. So I got her to put her legs up on the car bonnet (hood) just to see if she would do it. Of course, she did without hesitation. After our stretching, we set off down the path into the park, and I could see her strawberry blond hair glistening in the evening sun with her big blue eyes sparkling. I was getting hooked. After about three hundred feet, she halted and said,

"Hang on a minute, I have to stop." I instantly thought she had hurt herself and asked anxiously,

"What's the matter, are you okay!"

"I need a cigarette!" She then proceeded to take out a lighter and sparked up a Marlboro light! I could not stop laughing as we walked back to the car with Sarah happily puffing on her cigarette. At that moment, I knew she was the one. She was special. Anyone who knows Sarah will attest to that.

I was twenty-five and Sarah had just turned twenty. At the time, I was living at home with my parents. I remember coming home after that first date and sitting on my parents bed, which I had not done since I went off to boarding school at thirteen, and telling them,

"I've just met the girl I'm going to marry." I just knew she was the right one for me. I've always had this theory about relationships; everyone knows when it's not right, don't they? A year later we were married.

As I write this now, I knew at that moment when I first kissed you, Sarah, on that fallen tree in Dunham Park in the dead of the night that we would build a life together forever. There was always something unique about you, Sarah. You have this ability to light up a room. I would often sense a glow that would emanate from within you. It was this glow that attracted me to you. I realized over the years that this glow was actually your soul.

In the Jewish religion, we all have something called a N'shama, which literally means soul. I was sensing your soul. As you will see,

Sarah is my tether, my rock, and my partner through good and bad. She is my advocate through it all. Allowing me to stretch and follow my dreams and aspirations. She is my angel on my shoulder.

I wake up out of my daze as Sarah exclaims, "I wish I still smoked, I could do with a Marlboro Light right now!" as she winds down the window to let in some air into the stuffy car. Little did she know that I was just thinking about her pulling out those Marlboro lights on our first date nineteen years ago after we had run only a few yards. Lying with my head tilted to one side to keep the retina in place I start to smile and chuckle to myself. "What's so funny? How can you laugh at a time like this? I really need to find a convenience store and get some cigarettes!" she says with a cheeky smile on her face. I reach out and hold her hand as we did on that first date, and I squeeze it tight.

"Sarah, you have not smoked for seven years and *now* you want one? I just love the way you make me laugh. You're still that cheeky girl I met a long time ago in Dunham Park, aren't you?"

"Mmm, that's why you love me so much," she replies.

As we drive further and further into the desert, I start to drift off again and think about where I have come from and why this was happening to me, again. Have I not already endured enough? It is difficult to understand why I am in this precarious position. What is the meaning of it all?

Chapter 3: Seven

I had a very normal upbringing in rainy Manchester, England, with loving parents and two older brothers. I was lucky enough to have parents who always believed in me, encouraging and spurring me on to explore my own ideas and see them through. I was a very creative young boy, and I would always be drawing or making something. The visual world was my barometer, and I learned from a young age, with thanks to my father, that one should always look up and around when walking down the street. He'd tell me,

"Son, look at those buildings! Look at the details! There are too many people in this world that look down at their feet when they walk and they miss everything." He was right. People didn't seem to notice things like that. They were just too busy getting to their destination. I remember those buildings as we walked through the city of Manchester on our way to his office. The tall Corinthian pillars, the large stone Mullion windows, and the steep slate tile roofs. They were amazing, and I wondered what the people inside were doing as we walked and talked. He would hold my hand gently with his big soft hands. These days, he'd say they're looking at their phones! Little did I know what an impact those buildings would have later on in my life.

My dad is an entrepreneur through and through, and I presume that's how I caught the bug as well. He is not a big risk-taker, but a careful and considered man who has an eye for making money. He came from nothing, born into a family that had moved from Egypt in the 1930's after the family's cotton business had gone bust due to the Depression. Bust and broke, his parents brought him and his brother to Liverpool, England, to start afresh. The war soon came, and he was packed off to the countryside to live with another family to be out of harms way. He never talks about this so I don't know much more, but I am sure it was tough for him. He left school at sixteen and went straight to work, selling furniture on the markets. Soon, he worked his way up to working in furniture stores. His father was the manager of the local cinema in Liverpool, which I am told was quite a good job in those days. He eventually became manager of The Leicester Square Cinema for many years and met the Queen numerous times whenever the Cinema held a major film preview.

When I was born, my father began to prosper and acquired a number of the furniture shops he had worked in. He soon realized that the money was in the real estate, not the furniture. I did not see my dad too much growing up as he left for work early and came home late, but I do remember his strong features. I always thought he looked very similar to Sean Connery as James Bond when he was a younger man. He was actually even asked a couple of times for his autograph. My dad always liked a joke and sometimes pretended he was Connery and gave an autograph. On the weekends, he would often fall asleep under his newspaper after a long week of work while sitting in front of the television. I would try and tickle his toes, and he would always say he was awake and that he could see me through his newspaper. We would spend many Sundays playing cricket on our lawn at the front of the house, going out in his Jensen for a drive, or laughing as he wore goggles while cooking hamburgers on the barbecue. My mum, on the other hand, was always there caring for her three boys and making sure dinner was always on the table when my dad came home. She was the rock in our lives and allowed my father to reach his high aspirations. *As I write this, I am struck by how similar my family life is to my own upbringing. Subliminally, I assume we absorb this and look for that very comfort in our own lives.*

I was often in trouble as a child, and I honestly don't know how my parents put up with me. That's probably why I ended up at boarding school. At the age of seven, I tried my first cigarette—a Sobranie cocktail. They were all different colors, such as pink, yellow, blue, and green with gold tips that were placed in a small green marble box situated in what we called the "Best Lounge." The Best Lounge was a special room in our house only for adults and guests on special occasions. It had wall-to-wall carpet, vinyl silk wallpaper with a large fireplace, and very posh sofas. The cigarettes looked like sweets in a candy case, and I was lured to them, so no wonder, I tried one. I remember picking a blue one out of the marble box and putting it between my lips. I could smell and taste the tobacco. I played with it for a while, pretending to smoke it like I had seen people do on the television. I then saw a lighter on the small wooden table. It was made out of the same marble as the cigarette box, so I picked it up. It was heavy, and I pushed down on the brass ignitor, which revealed a flame. I looked around to check no one was coming and then dove behind one of the posh sofas and lit the end of the blue cigarette. It ignited instantly, and I sucked hard on the gold tip of the cigarette. The end glowed brightly and smoke started to billow from it as I coughed and sputtered out the smoke. I took another drag and once again coughed. My mouth tasted awful, and they certainly did not taste how they looked. I then proceeded to put out the cigarette on the plush carpet and throw the evidence away under the sofa.

It was not long before I got caught. Why would I think no one would see me (or smell me) smoking the cigarettes behind the sofa in the Best Lounge! Smoking was bad enough but to smoke them in the Best Lounge and then stub them out on the carpet, now that was just stupid, which only added to my stiff punishment.

Whenever I was in trouble, I used to have to go and wait in the Best Lounge until my father came home to dish out the appropriate punishment. The waiting was the worst punishment. However, I just realized, it was probably the waiting around that created my curiosity as I had plenty of time to look around and discover those cigarettes!

Seven was not a good year for me as it happens. One quiet Sunday afternoon, I "accidentally" burnt down the wooden greenhouse. My eldest brother had been peeling the paint off the keel of his beloved model sailboat with a candle. This was no ordinary model boat! It had large cloth sails that stretched about five feet in the air along a tall wooden mast. The boat was made from wood and had a wonderful yellow painted hue to it. There were real metal fasteners for the sails and real ropes. The deck was made from tiny pieces of maple wood stuck together to create a real deck finish. I always imagined that I could sail away in it to far-off places. On that fateful day, I was a bit bored and saw the model boat in the greenhouse, and I thought it would be a good idea to light the candle and see if I could help. Anyway, I must have forgotten to blow out the candle, so the greenhouse and my brother's beloved sailboat proceeded to burn down to the ground as we all watched "Ski Sunday" on the television. As smoke arose from the garden, everyone knew I had been up to mischief. There was pandemonium as my father tried to put out the fire with numerous fire extinguishers. My brother was screaming at me as he took the garden hose and doused down the flames. He could see his model sailboat was now ruined. "It was an accident!" I cried, "I was just trying to help. I'm so sorry!" My brother was distraught because he loved that boat, and I don't think he spoke to me for many months afterwards.

As usual, I was sent to the Best Lounge to await my punishment. I think my brother only really forgave me some thirty five years later when I came across a similar boat in a store in Coronado, California, not as big or as fancy as the original boat. I mailed it to him in England with the note, *sorry*.

The same week I burned down the greenhouse and turned my brother's boat to ashes I went to my mothers parents house, Jack and Joan Rubin's house for Shabbat[1] dinner. The shiny brass metal cap on the big red fire extinguisher in their downstairs toilet always fascinated me. I'm still not sure why the fire extinguisher was in there, but maybe, it was just for my enjoyment and pleasure.

After eating my chicken soup and challah[2], I decided to make a trip to the toilet. On that particular Friday night the lure of that shiny big brass metal cap was just too much for me. I investigated the cap for a moment and then discovered that I could lift the metal cap off, which was held in place by a brass chain and to my delight, I saw a large plunger underneath. I could not resist the temptation. I raised my right hand high above my head and hit the plunger as hard as I could. The next thing you know, *whoosh*, water was coming out of the end of the hose in a ferocious manner. I tried to control it, but it was to no avail. The whole bathroom was now soaked in foamy water, all of which only took a matter of seconds. The carpet was soaked, and the wallpaper was wet and starting to bubble.

I did not panic; I just flushed the toilet, replaced the brass metal cap on top of the fire extinguisher, and went back to the dining table to finish my meal, pretending nothing unusual had taken place. Some time later my grandma (or Grandy as we called her) went to the bathroom, and we were all greeted with a loud shriek of despair.

"Who's let off the fire extinguisher?" she cried. "Charles, you were just in there?"

I said nothing as I ate my strawberry Angel Delight and pretended that I had found it like that when I went in to use the toilet. "It must have been someone else?" I retorted. My grandfather just looked at me and gave me a wry smirk. It was similar to the smirk he had on his face a few months earlier when he decided it would be great

---

[1] Family dinner on the eve of the Jewish sabbath

[2] Platted bread eaten at the sabbath dinner

idea to show me how his 2.2 caliber World War Two pistol worked from his time as a Major in the British Army. We strolled down to the dark woods, which was located at the bottom of his garden. Once in the woods, he placed a target on a tree that he made out of paper and then proceeded to show me how to load the magazine. I was in heaven. He then gave me the gun and said,

"Just aim at that tree, my boy, and squeeze."

Crack, crack, crack—the gun went off as I hit the tree. A rush of excitement came over me as I continued to fire off the clip. *Crack, crack, crack*. We were giggling as he started to load up another magazine with the old bullets that were in his trouser pocket. Unfortunately for both my Grandfather and I, Grandy heard the loud noise and came running into the woods and saw me holding the gun with a huge smile on my face. "Look, Grandy, Papa is showing me how to shoot his World War Two pistol!" I exclaimed. She rushed over to us and scolded my Grandpa, making him hand over the smoldering weapon. She then ordered him to take the gun straight to the local police station, which he should have done after he returned from the war many years before. As the three of us headed out of the woods into the bright sunshine, he gave me a wink and squeezed my cheeks with his big soft hands and said,

"I'm in big trouble now." My grandfather loved my cheeky nature and would always stick up for me. He was a big man with a face that looked like Sir Winston Churchill. He was always smartly dressed with a dark blue blazer with gold buttons and a white or blue handkerchief in the top right pocket. We had a very close relationship, and I loved how he always let me ride on the running board of his old vintage car. I would hang on for dear life, as he would race down the private road outside his house. He would toot the horn as we went along, and I would have this huge smile on my face and tell him to go faster. I imagined I was in a gangster movie with a tommy gun, shooting imaginary bullets at the people taking a Sunday walk down the quiet, private street.

He would often tell me stories about the war and let me wear his old uniform, which was way too big for me. I didn't care; I just imagined I was a soldier as I played with his medals pinned to the jacket. On school holidays, he would take me to his office. He ran a large furniture business that had over a hundred stores, and I would go to his head office and play on the large switchboard which was a huge mass of wires and the switchboard operator would quickly move wires all over the place as she would connect the calls. On some special occasions, I was allowed to connect the calls myself. After playing around on the switchboard, I would meet him for lunch in the boardroom. Lunch traditionally consisted of fish and chips. We would sit at this huge polished wooden table that seated about twenty people in large leather chairs, but it would just be the two of us. The cook would bring in the food on a serving trolley and she would serve us. There were large bottles of ketchup and brown sauce on the table that we smothered the steaming hot chips with.

Occasionally, on a Saturday morning, he would take me to our small village railway station. He knew everyone and had a way with people. He even had probably paid the train operator to allow me to go up in the old railway house and change the points on the railway. He would stand behind me as I grabbed hold of this very large brown stick that projected from the floor and pulled it back towards me, which would change the points and move the approaching train onto the other track. I think he loved seeing the smile on my face as I moved this huge train from one side of the track to the other.

His true passion was horses and he owned many racehorses during his lifetime. We would often go to the races as a family and I would be allowed to bet on a horse and watch them race by and kick up the turf as they pelted around the track. I actually have a painting of him hanging on my wall in my office. My grandfather proudly standing next to his prize racehorse, which won the prestigious Grand

National[3]. I think we all have a connection with our grandparents, and I was certainly no exception. I loved Papa Jack.

My grandmother, Grandy, was the sweetest and most gracious lady I have ever known. She looked and behaved like the Queen. She was known to wear her signature trilby hat and smart blazer with pencil line tights on the beach in Marbella while carrying a parasol. Until the day my grandmother passed away, I would often go and visit her and have high tea at her house. This was a typical English afternoon tea with small cakes and sweet buns, and she would sit and listen to me with great intensity. She had many wonderful qualities, but her most undeniable feature was her ability to listen. Many people don't know how to listen, and she taught me that. While most people like to talk, she loved to listen to my stories and what I had been doing at school and later, when I was an adult. That tradition of high tea continued to the next generation as she re-created her own Victorian era childhood with her great grand children.

If you got on Grandy's bad side, she was a force to be reckoned with. I first experienced this during the fire extinguisher escapade when she shot me a look that I have never forgotten. That was enough for me to crumble and admit my wrongdoing. I also had sopping wet trousers, which were a pretty big giveaway.

It has just occurred to me that my grandfather actually looked like Sir Winston Churchill, and with my grandmother looking like the Queen, they could have made a fortune as a lookalike double act!

There were many other occasions when I got into mischief, such as the time I stripped off all the lead flashing on the garage roof with my friend Ben and sold it for scrap at the scrapyard in our local village.

---

[3] The Grand National is the great British Steeplechase horse race that has been running since 1893

You could say this was my first entrepreneurial idea. I think we got about four English pounds for our hard work. Carrying the heavy lead on our bicycles was not an easy task, I can assure you. My poor father realized something was up when water from the roof leaked on his Jensen. It cost him hundreds to repair. Not one of my best ideas! In the Best Lounge again to await my punishment!

I always had a fascination with roofs for some odd reason, and maybe it was due to the fact that I was always taught to look up at the buildings when I was a small child. I used to climb out of my parents' second floor bathroom window and ease myself carefully onto the parapet roof edge, which was about twenty-five feet up. I would then climb up onto the next roof and hide between the valley and just sit there for hours looking at the sky and daydream. This was very dangerous, which never occurred to me until I was much older.

Even now as I write about doing this, I really can't believe I did things like that.

I was fearless. I have always been fearless, continuing to look at life as a challenge. Even when I was at primary school, I remember thinking the teachers were no different from me and that I had a voice, which should be equal to theirs. As you can imagine, that was not always a good idea and it usually attracted a detention. There was one occasion, however, when my voice was heard. I was fed up with having to wear short trousers (or shorts) to school all year round. The winter was long in Manchester, and it was often very cold and wet; wearing shorts was not conducive to this harsh environment. I felt as if wearing shorts was outdated and Dickensian.

I decided to seek out the Headmaster, Mr. Mckay, and put my case forward for long trousers, especially in the winter. I knocked on his door and a stern voice from the inside said,

"Enter." There is something you should know about Mr. Mckay. He pretended to be a strict Headmaster, but he was really a kind and gentle man who played the drums. I loved the drums because my grandfather had bought me a set at age seven. I am not sure why I was rewarded with a set of drums at seven because I was not too well behaved that year. I think my grandfather did it as a joke to annoy my parents with the loud noise I would make. I went inside with an air of confidence and my head held high and exclaimed,

"I am fed up with wearing short trousers, sir!" McKay looked at me and tried to keep a straight face. The comment took him by surprise, but he allowed me to continue.

"Go on," he said.

"Well sir, it's freezing outside in the winter time, and I really don't understand why we can't wear long trousers in the winter and short trousers in the summer?" Simple and to the point, I thought. And in order to break the tension, I asked him how his new drum set was doing. He looked at me and said,

"Sidi, thank you for bringing this to my attention, but boys have been wearing short trousers at Altrincham Preparatory School for the past one hundred years." I looked at him and said bluntly,

"Well it's about time that changed then!" He tried not to laugh as he stroked his beard and explained that this was impossible to change. I left the room feeling quite dejected, but I knew I would not be defeated. Over the next week I got as many boys as I could to sign my petition. It was the "long trousers for winter" campaign.

I was soon back in his office, and I presented him with my petition. He took the paper and laid it to side of his desk.

"Thank you Sidi," he said, "now go back to class." One week later, he came into the classroom and announced that we no longer had to wear short trousers in the winter. I could not believe it. Everyone cheered, and at that moment, I knew I had a voice and was not afraid to use it. To this day, they still wear long trousers in the winter and shorts in the summer. It was my first victory.

Sadly, Mr. Mckay died some years later from cancer. I did not know what cancer was then and all I remember thinking was that I would not hear him play the drums again. He was the first of many advocates for me and I am truly grateful for his kindness and the chance he gave me to express myself. This was the first time I realized that determination and perseverance always prevail.

Chapter 4: On My Own

"Charles, are you okay?" Sarah says as she gently rubs my arm.

"Doing fine," I reply.

It is now 3:00 AM, and we are in the depths of the desert driving smoothly over the highway towards Yuma, Arizona. The road is perfectly straight as we pass semi-trucks trundling along, taking goods to their destination. It is a lonely road with nothing but the big dark sky and our car skimming through the air. We stop on the side of a dirt road, so I can go for a pee. I feel the warm air on my face as I look up at the stars. I feel so small and on my own, and I recall this is not the first time I have felt like this.

"Sidi, this is your bed here," said the older boy. I just looked at him and plopped down my bag and nodded. The bed had a scuffed white painted iron frame with a very thin lumpy mattress set amongst fifteen or so other lumpy beds. Some had teddy bears on them, and some had books. The dormitory was at the top of the boarding house with small windows overlooking a large playing field. I would spend many a night having to run around that playing field in my pajamas, even when it was snowing. This would be the usual punishment if the dorm were noisy at bedtime.

It was chaos with boys running around greeting each other and talking about their holiday break. I was thirteen and had just had my Bar Mitzvah some weeks before, and I was now at Polacks House at Clifton College boarding school. Clifton was about three hundred miles from Manchester and in the Southwest of the country.

Polacks[4] House was a boarding house for only Jewish boys in a school that was predominantly Christian and was first opened to Jewish boys in 1878. This was the only school of its kind in the country. We had our own synagogue in the house and kosher food. I joined Polacks half way through the school year and many of the boys had already made friends, so I was feeling quite alone. That was not the only thing that made me stand out. My Manchester accent was quite strong and many of the boys were from London, so I was quite the focus of attention. I was assigned a study, which was in the basement with two other boys. One was a great chap called Miles Webber. Miles and I have remained in touch over the years. I used to tease him and say he would be Prime Minister one day, as he could debate anything and would always win, which was very annoying. He was a bright and passionate student, and he would often help me with my homework. Not to my surprise, he went on to work for the Labour Party at the same time when a young man called Tony Blair was also working there. As many will know Tony Blair became Prime Minister. So I was close in my prediction but Miles decided to take another route and he was head hunted to work with Merrill Lynch as political advisor and since then moved on to become Head of U.K. External Affairs for General Electric Global Government Affairs as Operations Director. It's funny considering he was just my schoolmate who loved to listen to Wham and get drunk on Martini on the weekends. Joking aside, Miles was and still is a great friend and he taught me a lot about his beloved Israel, being a true Zionist.

---

[4] Polacks House Closed in 2005 as the Anglo Jewish community changed greatly and demand no longer supported the house.

He would fly the blue and white flag with the Star of David proudly in our study. I too started to love my religion and Israel at Polacks. I was not particularly religious at that time, Miles however was. He would often put on his tefillin[5] each day and I would be fascinated by it. For the past seven years I have put tefillin on each day and I am sure it was my schooldays and seeing Miles show me when I was young that influenced me. Our friendship and bond only deepened when we both went on summer camp to Israel, twice during our time at Polacks, experiencing life on Kibbutz where we picked cotton, smoked a lot of cigarettes and chased girls.

My early days at Clifton were lonely for quite sometime, and I remember being allowed to call my parents only once a week. The only telephone was situated in a small room next to the laundry room on the second floor. It had a green door, and inside were four white walls with a few scribbles on them and a wooden stool. The phone was an old fashioned pay phone that you would have seen in an English phone box. We had to put money in the phone or we could [6]reverse the charges.

"Mum, I want to come home," I said sniffling down the line, "I am home sick and everyone teases me about my accent." My mum would reassure me that everything was okay, and I would soon settle in. She was certainly right, but it was hard. I could not imagine having my boys go away to school at thirteen. I had recently talked to my mum about this as my son Adam has just gone to college at eighteen and that was hard enough with him simply being ten miles away. She explained that those phone calls were very hard for her too. She used

---

[5] Set of small black leather boxes containing scrolls of parchment inscribed with verses from the Torah, which are worn by observant Jews during weekday morning prayers. The arm-tefillin, or *shel yad*, is placed on the upper arm, and the strap wrapped around the arm, hand and fingers; while the head-tefillin, or *shel rosh*, is placed above the forehead.

[6] Call collect

to put the phone down each time and cry that her baby was away at school at such a young age. She knew, however, that it was going to all work out.

I would make the same call every week for months. As time went by, the calls became less and less frequent, and I eventually found my feet and started to enjoy school. I loved rugby and boxing. I decided it would be a good idea to join the boxing team because this would be a good way for me to assert my strength and avoid the bullying that went on at boarding schools. I was a natural, and I enjoyed the training and my teacher, who was an ex-professional named Gordon Hazel from the 1960's and was completely punch drunk. I could not understand a word he said to me, but boy, did he teach me how to box! I was junior school champion twice in a row. Everyone was my friend after that!

Clifton taught me to be independent and fend for myself at a young age. I could not seek advice from my brothers or parents as they were hundreds of miles away so we at the school learned to rely on our friends and to seek advice from our teachers. My friends became my family and we banded together and muddled through those forma-tive years. Once I had settled in, those first two years flew by, and I was now fifteen and assigned to a room with just one other boy named Alex Lee, who turned out to be a second cousin of mine. Alex now lives in Australia with his family. Many of us from Polacks have traveled the world and moved to new countries. I sincerely believe that Polacks was the cause for that. None of us were afraid; we all had dreams and were all taught to pursue them.

Rosh Hashanah[7] and Yom Kippur[8] came and went, and winter passed quickly. It was soon to be Passover[9] and time to go home. I remember going to bed one night feeling a little heavy-hearted. I did

---

[7] Jewish New Year

[8] Jewish Day of Atonement

[9] Jewish festival remembering the exodus of the jews from Egypt

26

not know why, but I had an awful feeling in my stomach. The next morning, I was woken up by my Housemaster Dr. Hershon. I liked Dr. Hershon, he was a kind man with a big heart and would often give me the benefit of the doubt when other boys were not that lucky. It wasn't until later that I truly appreciated his kindness and support.

"Charles, wake up. Charles, I have to tell you....." I interrupted him and said,

"I know, it's okay. He's dead isn't he?" He looked at me strangely and said,

"How do you know? I am sorry, but your grandfather has died." I just knew; I had a strong feeling, and I felt physically sick. My grandfather Jack was gone. I could feel his big, soft hands squeezing my cheeks. His love of racehorses and his love for his grandchildren would be no more.

I packed a small bag and made my way to the train station. I took the train from Bristol Temple Meads Station to Stockport Station in the north, close to Manchester. I had made this journey many times, but this one was different. The sky was dark, and it was a typical rainy day, but this time, it felt as if the clouds seemed to follow me from school to my house in the suburbs of Manchester. My heart was so heavy. I had never been to a funeral before, and I was nervous. My Mum picked me up at the station, and I still remember her face to this day. She looked so pale because she had lost her father. She was trying to be brave, but I knew she was so sad inside. She gave me a smile, and we traveled silently in the car to our home. It was a lovely place with a big long sweeping drive set amongst old oak trees that I used to climb and play in. As I arrived at the house, it looked a lot smaller than I had remembered it; the old patch of ground where the greenhouse that had burnt down many years before was now a beautiful garden. I walked into the house, and I saw my father on the telephone in his office. This was no ordinary office but a very large room that was lined with oak panels, two fireplaces, and a huge semi-circular vaulted ceiling. My father's desk was set right in the middle of the room with two large sofas in front of one of the fireplaces and a billiard table behind his desk. It sounded like he was talking to the funeral director and organizing what was to be an experience that I have never forgotten.

Jewish funerals are not pleasant occasions.

I stood with my brothers and my parents in a prayer room. The prayer room looked like an old schoolhouse building with a vaulted roof with a single lamp hanging from the tall ceiling that barely lit the room. It was a cold March day, so it was freezing in there, full to the brim with family and friends paying their respects as the rain came clattering down on the clay tiled roof. I caught myself looking at my grandfather's coffin, which was just a plain plywood box, overlain only with a Tallit[10]. Being Jewish, the coffins are very basic and are to replicate how we come in to this world. We came with nothing, so we leave with nothing. My grandfather was a fairly big man, and I just kept thinking that the box looked too small for him to be in there. I could not help but think about whether he would be wearing his navy blazer with gold buttons and pressed handkerchief in his upper right pocket or his Army uniform and medals. In fact, some years after he died, I was given his medals in a frame, and they hang in my bathroom. I could not get the image out of my head of him being squeezed into that tiny box. I felt the tears streaming down my face as we started to say the Mourners Kaddish[11]. The prayer room was obviously not equipped with heating, and it was so cold my toes were beginning to go numb. Once the prayer service was over, we filed out and followed the coffin which was headed slowly to the grave. Out of the corner of my eye, I could see my mum gripping my dad's arm as he held her firmly. I was walking between my two older brothers,

---

[10] Jewish prayer shawl

[11] Jewish prayer said for the dead usually at a funeral service

and they were both weeping. As we walked closer and closer to the grave, the dark deep hole seemed to get bigger and bigger as we approached. *There it is, the hole they are going to put him in.* I thought.

The pallbearers awkwardly lowered the box into the grave, and it shifted from side to side until it met its resting place with a gentle thud. It was now raining and everyone was standing around the grave under their umbrellas. I'm looking down at him in that small box in the bottom of the grave, trying to remember all the great things we had done together. It was just blank though, and I could not focus on anything else except the box in the ground. As we all stood there, and the Rabbi started to pray I was so focused on the box I felt his soul rise up from the ground, and I followed it up to the dark sky as the rain drops splattered on my face. That was the same soul I would feel many years later when my first child Adam *Jack* Sidi was born. I talked to you that day, Jack, when Adam was born and I remember it to this day. Adam was at the beginning of his life and all I could tell him that I wished you had met him. You would have loved squeezing his cheeks.

The sound of the dirt being shoveled on the coffin jolted me and lifts me from my trance. I am handed a shovel to do my duty. It is a Mitzvah[12] in the Jewish religion to bury the dead and cover the coffin completely. I walk up to the grave and shovel some dirt gently onto the coffin, and I will never forget that sound as it hit the roof of the plywood box with a thud!

I am startled by the car door thud as Sarah gets back in the car. "Charles, come on. We need to get going" she shouts at me as I do up my trousers and stumble back into the car. "Are you alright? You look like you've seen a ghost. You look so pale?" she continues.

"Yes, I'm fine. I was just thinking about stuff," I reply.

"Hmm, what stuff?" she mumbles.

---

[12] Act of human kindness

The car trundles off the dirt road, kicking up stones as we head back onto the highway. I put on the radio and channel surf for a few minutes to try and change the mood and avoid Sarah asking me any more questions. To my surprise, "Careless Whisper" by George Michael is on, which reminds me of my life at school once again.

I was not the perfect student, and I was still rather carefree. However, losing my grandfather woke me up, and I realized it was time to make something of myself. I started to listen in class and actually found out that I was good at absorbing information. Not only did I enjoy learning, I wanted to help out the younger kids at the school. When I first arrived at Polacks, I was the only boy from Manchester. Soon, there was quite a number of us. I guess I was a bit of trail blazer. There was one particular lad, Robin, who had had some trouble with bullying. I had also been bullied at my previous school and had endured two years of abuse from a boy, so I knew what it was like to be lonely and scared.

I told Robin that the only way to deal with a bully is to stand up to them. He was quite a timid lad at that time, and I am sure he cried to his parents in that phone box just like I did. In the end, I intervened and told the bully to back off, or I would take him in the boxing ring and teach him a lesson. That's how we did things back then. Not quite the way it's done these days, but it was effective. The boy backed off, and Robin was able to once again enjoy school and prosper. It was a small thing, and I thought nothing of it. When I left school some years later, Robin's father gave me my first real job working in his company. He was so grateful for me helping his son that he felt indebted to me. His company made kitchen and bedroom furniture, and I worked in the design studio, designing kitchen layouts and creating the manuals of how the items went together. Think very early IKEA. We had to illustrate everything and draw the designs by hand, even down to the different size screws that showed how the cabinets were held together. There were no computers to assist us, just a steady hand. That job meant so much to me, and I still use many of those skills today.

Even though I had started to take school more seriously, I was still a teenager and could not help but get myself into trouble. Every so often, we would have a fire drill in the house and this had two purposes. The first was to make sure that everyone could get out of the house in one to two minutes in case of an actual fire, and the second was to catch people who were out of the house when they shouldn't be. I remember on one particular occasion, it was a Saturday night and I wanted to go and see my girlfriend who was a pupil at the sister school to Clifton. I had made sure that my friends knew I was going out just in case there was a fire drill.

"Miles, I am going to see Nikki tonight. Can you call my name out if there is a drill?" He accepted the responsibility, and I headed out. A few hours later, I remember the phone ringing at the house of my girlfriend. We did not have mobile phones in those days, so it seemed strange that someone would be calling after midnight. I heard Nikki's parents pick up the phone and say,

"I don't think he would be here at this time of the night, Dr Hershon." My heart sank and I thought, *Oh shit, I'm in big trouble now.*

There was indeed a fire drill that night, and everyone got out of the house in record time. They started the roll call, and it soon got to my name. Dr. Hershon called out my name, and there was a slight pause, and then apparently three of my friends all replied for me in quick succession from different parts of the quad. It was now very obvious I was not at the house. All three of my friends were brought into Dr. Hershon's study and interrogated. They soon caved in and told him where I was. Nikki's father was not impressed, as you can imagine. I was not supposed to be at his house with his daughter anyway. I ran as fast as I could all the way back to the house. I knew this was not going to be good. I arrived at the house out of breath, and Dr. Hershon was standing on the front steps of the house with a very stern look on his face.

"Sidi, get in the house and go straight to bed. Come and see me tomorrow at 7:00 AM and don't be late!" he shouted.

I scuttled off to bed, knowing what would await me in the morning. I did not get too much sleep that night. The following morning I was at his study by 6:55 AM, awaiting my punishment.

"You know the rule, Charles, if you are caught not attending a fire drill, don't you?" he asked calmly.

"Yes sir" I replied.

"Two weeks detention after school in my study with extra homework and no sports or free time." I accepted my punishment and the next two weeks ended up going by very slowly.

As I explained, Dr. Hershon could have been much harder on me, but for some reason, he believed in me and would often provide encouragement. I liked him, and we had a mutual respect for each other. Many years after I left Clifton and was married with my first son Adam, I did some research and managed to find his telephone number. I had heard that he was in not too good health and had long since been Housemaster at Polacks. I decided to call him.

"Dr. Hershon, this is Charles Sidi. How are you?" I began. The phone line was quiet for a moment as I could hear he was processing the name he had not heard for ten years.

"Charles, is that you? So lovely to hear from you!" he said in a frail voice. We spent the next thirty minutes talking and I told him about all things I was doing and thanked him profusely for believing in me, encouraging me, and providing me with so many second chances. He laughed and said he always knew I would turn out all right. I was so pleased to be able to tell him that I really appreciated his kindness and caring nature towards me, and that his job was certainly not in vain. He passed away a few weeks after that call. I would hope to think he was happy to know that he had made an impact on his students and provided us with encouragement, as well as the boundaries we all needed.

You would have thought that that fire drill punishment would have deterred me from missing another one; well, you'd be wrong. A few months later, a friend of mine in the year above named Roger decided it would be a great idea to go on a little trip for the weekend. We had it all planned out military style. Leave the house after synagogue on Saturday morning and sign out of the house as normal and have someone else sign us both back in later that day so Dr. Hershon would think we were in the house. As soon as synagogue was over, we ran into our rooms and got changed out of our school uniforms into our casual clothes. We then ran to the bus stop and took the bus to Bristol Temple Meads train station. Roger and I were laughing and thinking how easy this was. We bought two return tickets to Birmingham, about an hour and half to the north, where his parents lived. His parents were away that weekend, so we had complete run of the house and use of his father's cars!

Think Ferris Bueller's Day off! This film had just aired (1986), and we thought it was so cool. We arrived at Roger's parents' house, and we watched a bit of TV and played some pool. It would not be long before I was standing in his father's garage confronted by a shiny red Porsche 928. It looked fantastic and Roger said cheekily, "Let's take it for a spin, shall we?"

"Fuck yes!" I said, and we both buckled in while Roger took the wheel. It was crazy. There I was playing truant from school, hundreds of miles away, and Roger is now driving down the M6, South towards London at 1:00 AM. He was not just cruising; he was flooring it. At one point I looked at the speedometer, and we hit 160mph. It was so fucking fast that the broken lines that divide the lanes on the motorway had now formed one perfect straight line. The world was going by so fast; it was almost a blur. My heart was pounding and I was terrified. "Slow down!" I screamed at Roger and he just looked at me and laughed and continued to floor it.

We made it to London in record time and went to a night club to meet up with some girls that Roger knew. One was a sweet girl named Fleur, who was Roger's girlfriend at the time. Roger married Fleur some years later. We left early in the morning and drove back to Birmingham to deliver the car safely back from whence it came. Fortunately, it did not end like Ferris Bueller's Day off. The car was returned without a mark, and I don't believe his father ever knew what we had done. We took the train back to school that afternoon wondering if we had been caught out or if there had been a fire drill. Leaving school like that was punishable by expulsion.

It was our lucky weekend, no one knew we were gone and Roger and I laughed about this for years, and still do. It was completely irresponsible, and I have often thought about how dangerous and stupid it was, but there was no doubt it was a lot of fun!

There was a darker side to Clifton that I still, to this day, can't believe actually went on and was actually approved by the faculty. When the new boys would arrive each year, they would be subjected to something called "Night Ops." It was a tradition at the school that all the freshman (only 12-13 years old) would be woken up in the middle of the night, and told to get dressed as quickly as possible and were then given instructions of what would happen next. Clifton was well known for the Clifton Suspension Bridge that spanned the Cheddar gorge, a deep valley in the landscape with a river running at the bottom of it. This is where our 'Night Op" would take place. For the next five hours, in the dark cold night, we would be subjected to abuse and discomfort. I am not entirely sure why this was a tradition, apart from the fact that it was a rite of passage of some sort. It was barbaric and outdated.

Fortunately, if you remember I was already on the boxing team and this most certainly helped me avoid some of the awful things that went on. We set off on our "treasure hunt" down into the deep dark gorge with just torches[13], shivering as we descended into the

---

[13] Flashlight

34

dark valley. Suddenly, we were confronted by the first group of older boys waiting in the darkness. At one time, they had also been subjected to a similar or worse experience, and it was now their turn to dish out the punishments. "Get down on the ground!" they shouted at us. As I dropped to the cold stony wet floor, the smell of the wet moss stung my nostrils as my face crumpled against the stones on the ground. I looked up and saw that they were all dressed in combat fatigues. As part of our curriculum, all boys had to take part in the Army Cadets at school, learning to march in the quad, clean our boots to a perfect shine until you could see your own reflection in them and learn how to shoot rifles and more. I actually loved the Cadets as it was a great discipline and being allowed to shoot a weapon at thirteen was a lot of fun.

Suddenly I could smell something strange and I felt warm water being poured onto me, it felt warm against the cold night air, but I quickly realized that older boys had started to pee on us. I felt a reflex in my throat and started to gag. One poor boy was chosen out of the group and made to drink a glass of piss. He resisted at first but was then beaten until he did. *As I write this now, I can't believe how disgusting this whole process was,* but at the time, I was just thinking survival. Once this initial hazing was over, we were told to go further down into the gorge, after which they confiscated our torches. We were all terrified, just clinging to each other as we could not see as we brushed against branches and thorns from the trees lining the dark windy path. We were confronted by different groups for the next few hours being subjected to just plain bullying. A number of the boys in the group were now crying, and it was matter of just keeping it together. The last stage of the "Night Op" was soon upon us. There it was; the tunnel. We had all heard about this from the older boys for the preceding months but it was not until we were actually faced with walking through this old disused railway tunnel that stretched at least half a mile did we really understand fear.

It had been some four hours since we had been woken up from our warm beds, and we were now walking down this pitch-black tunnel that was so cold and wet. You could smell the old tar that had been long since painted on the railroad sleepers underfoot, which also made it difficult to keep your balance. All I could see was my cold breath in front of my face as the cold night air whipped through the tunnel and made me shiver. You could have heard a pin drop in there, it was so quiet. From all of the previous hazing, we were so tired and scared, fear had completely taken over. We were all shaking and no one said a word. After a few hundred yards, we decided to move to the side of the tunnel so we could use the walls for balance. I could feel the slimy walls as my hands brushed against them. We were now all gripped to each other in a long line. Alex was at the front of the group as he led us further and further into the tunnel. We were now about halfway through the tunnel, and we could just about see some light at the other end as it was just beginning to get light. It was not too far now I thought, and it would soon be over. Just get through this and we would be home free.

Suddenly my friend Alex screamed out loud, "I've been shot, fuck! My leg, I've been shot!" There was complete panic and pandemonium. We all dived to the ground as fast as we could. I tripped over one of the sleepers and stumbled to the ground, scuffing my hands to break my fall. Alex was screaming in the background as his voice reverberated around the tunnel. The loud noise startled all the bats that had been lining the tunnel roof. What seemed like hundreds of them scuttled out of the tunnel above our heads. Thank goodness it was still quite dark so I could not see them.

One of the older boys thought it would be funny to take his air rifle and shoot at us as we walked down the tunnel. It was fucking unbelievable. I was so mad and had completely had enough of this bullshit. I just got up an ran as hard as I could at the older boys screaming at them, "What the hell are you doing?! You're all insane!" Clearly the older boys were now worried as they were going to find it pretty difficult to explain how one of the younger boys had been SHOT.

We all headed back to the house as the sun was starting to come up allowing us to warm our tired cold bodies. We carried Alex back to the house where the house nurse proceeded to clean up his wound. As you can imagine, Dr. Hershon was not happy, so the boys involved were in deep trouble. This was the last time a "Night Op" ever occurred. The tradition was over.

As time went by I discovered that my favorite subject at school was art. I loved to draw and paint, and I was also good at building stuff. In my last year at school, I persuaded my teachers that it would be a good idea for me to spend all day at the art school, which was unheard of. No student had ever managed to do this. I am not saying that this was a great idea, but again it was testament to my vision and my persuasive nature. When I get an idea, nothing seems to get in my way. My passion came through and no one wanted to dash that. So there I was taking only art classes in my final year at school. My friends could not believe it. Of course, I graduated that class with an A.

I decided to leave school early at seventeen, as I felt I needed something more. Clifton had served me very well, but it was time for me to move on. I graduated with nine O Levels[14] and 1 A level[15]. Not bad, I thought. I came back to Manchester and attended a community college and studied Sculpture and Foundation Art, which I passed with flying colors. Again I wanted more, so I decided to attend another college to study chartered surveying. I enjoyed the practical stuff, but the theory and math were not my favorite. After a year, I moved to London to continue my studies and gain some work experience. My dad had got me a job working for a friend of his called

---

[14] General Certificate of Education taken by students at the age of 15

[15] Advanced Certificate of Education taken by students at the age of 18

Bob Dyson at his commercial Real Estate Agency. There I was again, alone and starting something new. I lived in my brother's apartment in South Kensington. I would meet up with Roger and his new wife Fleur on a number of occasions, and we would laugh about all the stupid things we did at Clifton.

Bob was great guy, a typical commercial agent. I used to take the tube to Green Park, near Central London, everyday and I would go out on different assignments. I did not really enjoy it, but Bob really tried to help me. I remember him taking me out with clients for many boozy lunches, which were quite an eye opener. That was the way business was done then, I suppose.

About a year ago my dad passed me a letter that Bob had written to my dad after I had decided to leave Dunlop Heywood some twenty four years earlier.

I could not believe what I read. Clearly here was another person in my life who believed in me and was yet another advocate for me.

Flat Two
91, Ouslaw Gardens
London SW7 3BU
18th January 1990

Dear David,

Thank you for your letter. I tried to call you on a couple of occasions for a brief word, but without success.

I know you will be disappointed that Charles does not, for the moment, find the wonderful property business as appealing as you do.

But fear not, and if I may be so bold, Charles is a great guy, he won me over at his interview not because he was David Sidi's son but because he presented himself properly, showed enthusiasm (perhaps not, as it transpires, for property, but as a person) and convinced me he would have a good go.

I have got to know Charles reasonably well in the past few months and whilst I have to admit he is not as stimulated (words lost here) you or me he has all sorts of qualities not least the best being the inimitable Sidi charm.

He was particularly well thought of by his colleagues and was a helpful, friendly member of my London office. Moreover, I think it was quite something for him to come and put his cards on the table, in the sure knowledge that you would not be jubilant.

We all look forward to seeing^him in Chamonix next week and I have no doubt that he will find success in whatever field he elects to enter- you never know he may come around to thinking property wasn't that bad after all!!

David, he is a smashing sort and you need not worry at all.
Best Regards

Bob Dyson

Flat Two,
91, Onslow Gardens,
London SW7 3BU.

18th, January, 1990.

Dear David,

Thank you for your letter. I tried to call you on a couple of occasions for a brief word, but without success.

I know you will be disappointed that Charles does not, for the moment, find the wonderful property business as appealing as you do.

But, fear not, and if I may be so bold, Charles is a great guy; he came over at his interview, not because he was Saint Silk's son but because he presented himself properly, showed enthusiasm (perhaps not, as it transpires, for property) but as a person) and convinced me he would have a good go.

I have got to know Charles reasonably well in the past few months and whilst I have to admit he is not as stimulated you or we he has all sorts of qualities not the least being the invincible Bill Cheam.

He was particularly well thought of by his colleagues and was a helpful, friendly member of my London office. Moreover, I think it was quite something for him to come and put his cards on the table, in the sure knowledge that you would not be jubilant.

We all look forward to seeing him in Aramania next week and I have no doubt that he will find success in whatever field he elects to enter — you never know he may come around to thinking properly, wasn't that bad after all !!

David, he is a smashing sort and you need not worry at all.

Best Regards,

Well Bob, how prophetic you were! About a year after this letter was written, I found my first development deal, and I was just nineteen. Little did I know that I would spend the next twenty plus years building a career for myself as a property developer. So much for my dad having to worry about me not being interested in real estate!

As I reflect upon my years at Polacks House I am convinced that those formative years are so much a part of my very being. I to this day believe that Polacks has played a significant part in my later life. At such a young age I was thrust into a place where I had to make connections quickly and learn to communicate while at the same time try to get my point of view across. All of which has played a role in my work and personal life. The bonds and friendships that were made there were cast in stone and each one of us have gone forward with a true understanding of others, self belief and determination.

Chapter 5: Human Doings

I t is now 4:00AM, and we are getting close to Yuma, Arizona. Sarah is waning, and tiredness is setting in. The adrenaline that pumped through our veins has worn off, and she has run of out of coffee. It is dark and our headlights guide the way through the desolate highway. I know we are now in Arizona because I can feel the heat transfer through the window of the car. This reminds me that we are getting closer to Phoenix, and the feeling of freedom has quickly disappeared. We aren't just on a drive through the night, but on a drive of desperation to save my sight.

I feel very nervous about my surgery. I know what is to come and my mind is going into a downward spiral. What will I do without my sight? How will I be able to earn a living and keep my family afloat? The last five years have been very tough, in terms of business, with the global economic downturn, and I have not been immune to that. It has only been a couple of years since I started my new business with Rick, and it is proving to be very difficult to get off the ground. I can feel the stress start to build and my heart is skipping a beat.

"I'm so sorry," I tell Sarah, who is startled by my voice as I had been quiet for the past hour. I am pretty sure she thought I was asleep.

"Sorry for what?" she replies.

"I'm sorry for bringing you to America and making you start all over again. Sorry for putting you through all the tough times we have had," I say.

"Don't be silly Charles. You're just feeling vulnerable at the moment and now is not the time to be thinking like that." she states sternly. She is right, but so am I. I am sorry for making her leave her family and our friends in England seven years ago to start a new life in America. It has been a very tough transition for all of us, but specifically for Sarah. She left all her family in the UK and was now faced, once again, with looking after me. But this time, she could be looking after someone who could lose his independence. This is a tall order for both of us.

"What are we going to do if I can't see?" I ask, "How are we going to cope with that?" Sarah doesn't reply as she keeps her eyes on the road. She does not want to go there; she wants to remain positive. I know she is just being brave and trying to stay calm, but inside, she is scrambling, trying to keep her head above water.

Sarah is brilliant in a crisis, but the after effects of this situation were always tough. She gives everything and more. Once the crisis is over, it's only natural to fall apart. I found that out myself some months later.

As human beings, I think we all do a great job of holding it together on the outside; however, on the inside, we are falling apart. Sometimes the well becomes too full, and we overflow. I think we should be called "human doings," not human beings. We seem to spend so much time doing and not enough being. I am guilty of this more than anyone because I have spent my whole life doing.

I have learned through this very tough experience that it's vital to just "be" and let life take its course. We can't control everything; we are mere co-pilots in this life. We reach many crossroads in life, and as my dad would say to me, "It's how you proceed that matters. Choose a road and stick to it."

44

It took me a long time to find my true self, and the prospect of losing my sight was a big part of that process. You think you have it all together—wife, two children, good career, friends, family, and then one day out of the blue...a fucking train hits you and not just once, but time and time again. I just kept getting back up, yet each time I would be knocked back down just like a boxer. I dealt with a variety of things, whether it was struggling to build a business or dealing with health issues. It is not until you realize that it's actually the small things that really have an impact when one of your senses is removed. Not being able to drive, to see your children's faces, to see in order to shave, to see the leaves on the trees, to see the mountains, to watch a movie or a television show. You start to notice that your hearing gets better and your senses alter to compensate for the lack of vision. You live in a world on your own, in a bubble. Then, the human body learns to adapt and survival takes over. I learned how to make the words on my computer huge so I could read them; I used a magnifying glass to read emails. I would get a ride to the gym and get picked up afterwards, a ride to work and then home again, a ride to the eye doctor for check ups where I would see many others with the same problem and worse.

My independence was fading fast and I was desperately fighting inside to become a human doing again. It seemed like the natural thing to do. I wanted more than anything to be independent and drive my car and watch my boys play soccer. I couldn't; so for the first time in my life, I stopped and became a human being. Recognizing that life is much more than just doing. Doing stuff for the sake of doing is just bollocks. It is in our nature just to do, we spend so much time wasting time. Businesses have meetings for the sake of meetings, creating work for themselves that is not necessary and creating a structure that is based on doing. We all end up paying for that; we just end up paying for someone else's waste. If we are producing something, it feels as if we are at achieving. The majority of the things we do are just to fill time, and we don't use our time wisely in a meaningful way. If we all just stopped for a while and recognized the true meaning of being, then we would be a much more considered and efficient human race.

How many times do we hear people say "I hate Mondays?" Thinking like that means that one seventh of your life is wasted? Mondays are just as much of a gift as Fridays; it's just how you view it. How many times do we say, "what shall we do today?" How about we stop and say, "what shall we be today?"

Chapter 6: Fearless Or Rose Colored Glasses

Youth, beautiful youth
We walk through walls until we find the truth
and then change it.

George Michael

Even though I am nervous and frightened about what is to come, I remember a time when fearlessness seemed natural to me. Being young and wearing "rose colored glasses" also helped a lot.

"Dad, I have found something amazing! It's two old derelict barns built in the 1820's," I said to him through the car phone. It was like a brick with numbers on the back that made a noise when you pressed them.

"Go on," he said.

"I have a vision for making two upscale homes. The buildings have great character, and they are set back from the road with an old cobbled courtyard," I declare excitedly.

I had never built anything before, and I was just nineteen years old. I had no real knowledge of how to go about building. I just knew what I wanted to do with them. I could see the buildings finished in all their glory. I have always had this ability to visualize the end product and make it happen.

A few months before, I worked in an architectural office for a great guy named Neil Collins. He was kind enough to give me an internship and show me the ropes. I had taken my skills from the kitchen company and was now applying them to houses. This opportunity greatly excited me, and I even had my own drawing desk. Each day, I would work on plans and elevations, drawing them to scale on a piece of tracing paper with a 0.5mm Rotring pen with black ink. It took a certain skill to make sure the ink did not run and create different thicknesses for lines that illustrated building features. If you made a mistake, you could not just rub it out. You had to use a razor blade and physically scratch it out, making sure not to tear the tracing paper.

Architecture has always fascinated me since the days when my father would show me the buildings on his way to his office. I remember one particular morning when he took me to an architectural office called Stephenson Bell. A tall silver-haired man named Roger Stephenson ran the practice. They had been working with my father for many years on a number of projects. I remember his office was a converted schoolhouse in an area of Manchester called Castlefield, which had many old buildings and Roman ruins. The office was a hive of activity with drawing boards as far as the eye could see. Stephenson Bell had converted the office inside into a very modern and minimalist space, combining the old and new. It was very cool, and I always thought it would be great to work there.

I am not sure if it was the letter from Bob Dyson that spurred my dad on or not, but when he saw that I was finally excited about property, he very kindly agreed to loan me the money to buy the two derelict barns and develop them. My dad truly believed in me, and it was a testament to the fact that he let me take control of the whole process from start to finish. We did have weekly meetings to go over budgets and design, which he loved and gave me accountability.

The first thing I needed was an architect and I knew exactly who to call.

"Neil, it's Charles Sidi. How are you?" I continued,

"I've bought two old barns, and I am going to develop them under my company, Planetree Properties," I said enthusiastically. Planetree was a company my father had started some years earlier, and I took on this company name for what ended up being the next fifteen years. The phone was quiet for a moment, but then he questioned,

"Sorry Charles, you've bought two what?"

"Two barns! They have so much character, and I want you to be the architect." I think he was stunned.

In a matter of months, I'd gone from an intern to a property developer orchestrating the whole show. Imagine, I was just nineteen and I was now employing sub-contractors, architects, engineers and setting up accounts with local suppliers and agreeing contracts. It was a trial by fire. I learned on the job.

I was up and running on the site in all weathers from 7:00 AM until 7:00 PM. I was buying materials, as well as designing the kitchens, bathrooms, and room layouts. Skills I had previously learned were coming into play. I was desperate to prove not only to myself, but also to my father that I could make my vision a reality. This project was like going to university for me. Although I had no teachers, I just immersed myself in the task and listened and watched the tradesmen do their jobs. One day, I would be taking slate tiles off the roof and the next, digging ditches for the drains. Everyday there was something new. It was an incredibly creative process from start to finish. I remember sitting on the apex of the roof when we had finished installing all the new slates and looking out over the houses for miles around. I felt free and the feeling of accomplishment was tangible.

I was not intimidated by anything or anyone; not even the burly bricklayers that were twice my age and size scared me. I remember one occasion when the "brickies," as we called them, wanted to leave early on a Friday to go to the pub. I was so frustrated that my job had to stop in order for these guys to go home and get drunk. One day, I approached them and told the 300 lb. leader of the gang, "Lads, if you leave early today you're not getting paid." He looked at me like I had two heads and shoved his trowel in my face and shouted,

"Are you fucking joking?!" I stood firm and said,

"No, I'm serious." At that point, he proceeded to take a swing at me and in this moment, all that training with my boxing coach Gordon Hazel a few years earlier came quickly into action. I ducked and he missed me completely, while all the other lads on the site started laughing. It must have been quite comical. I was this little scrawny young lad squaring off with this big burly bloke. Bloody fearless.

The lads still went to the pub and of course, I still paid them. But after that incident, they all respected me, and I learned that you have to stand up to whoever or whatever is bothering you. Never be intimated by others.

As the weeks and months went by, the barn was coming to life. I felt myself breathing life back into these old buildings, and I was loving every minute of it. I could finally express myself in a way that was creative and profitable. The barns were finished about a year later, and I moved into one of the houses. I called it The Shires because Shire horses had been housed there for many years. I lived there for the next ten years. I loved that house and still do. Sarah and I moved in after we got married and started to raise Adam and Joshua there.

We changed quite a few things in the house and made it our first home. It turned out to be so nice that it was featured in a magazine called Cheshire Life.

Chapter 7: "Building" A Career

I was now twenty-six, and Adam had just been born. I was in full swing as a property developer. I had started to make a name for myself in the industry as the "Barnstormer". After my first foray with The Shires, I saw a niche in the market and started to buy up old barns in the area and turn them into high-end homes. I had a great eye for seeing things that others couldn't. Where others saw old, derelict buildings, I saw beauty, design, and profit.

"Harry, I've found another one! It's fantastic, got the biggest roof in Cheshire," I exclaimed on my cell phone. "I am here now standing outside of it. We can bring it back to life," I continued. Clearly, I had a thing for roofs.

Harry Calder was a young architect that had started his practice in Manchester a few years prior and wanted to burn up the world and make something of himself, similar to me. Harry was a little older than I and liked a pint or two, and we would often sit in the pub and discuss the next development. He was and still is a brilliant architect with a great eye for detail and design flair. We played off each other's strengths, and I was willing to give him the reigns to my vision. It was a great collaboration and I knew he would be perfect for the job.

"Charles, Where is it?' he asked excitedly.

"It's Gawsworth Hall," I said.

"Fuck me!" he cried out in his strong Scottish accent. "I'm on my way." Within the hour, he had arrived. We spent the afternoon looking around a huge Grade 2* Listed barn that was over 20,000 sq. ft in size. (A Grade 2* Listed building is one of the highest protected buildings by the Government for architectural merit and character.)

The walls were five feet thick, and the oak trusses that held up the stone roof dated back to the 14th century. The place was full of pigeons and their excrement, yet we didn't care. "I know exactly what were going to do with this, Charles," Harry stated. "Four fucking great big houses, within the walls of this treasure," he went on merrily. A few months, later it was mine and the work had started.

This was no small undertaking, both financially and physically. I was not only the developer, but also the site foreman. I spent the next two years working out of a cold site cabin ordering materials, doing accounts, designing and coordinating multiple trades. It was definitely a tough process, but I loved it. I have always cared deeply about all the projects I have worked on, and this one was no exception. Since it was a protected building, we had to work very closely with the government to maintain the integrity of the building according to their exacting specifications. This meant that any bricks, which needed replacing with new ones, had to match with the old ones. They had to match not only in color, but also in the way they were "fired," as if they were made three hundred years ago. The mortar that held it all together had to be made from lime and horsehair. You can't learn this from the books, only from being "hands on."

As you recall, this was the largest roof in Cheshire. It had over five hundred tons of York stone flag tiles on the roof some as big as 5 ft. by 3 ft. One of the first things that attracted me to this building proved to be my first real lesson in development. I employed a sub-contractor who had the lowest price to strip the roof and replace it, after we repaired it's old support structure. The contractor stripped the roof and numbered all the large stone flags, which were now all off the roof in the field next to the barn. There were thousands of pieces. We then proceeded to repair the roof as planned. Some weeks later I got a phone call.

"Charles, it's John from the roofing company," the voice said. "Well, I've got some bad news." My heart sank and my stomach flipped.

"What is it now?" I questioned. I had a bad feeling about this company from the start, but as my dad told me many times: pick a road and stick to it.

"We're not coming back to the job; we simply can't afford to put the roof back on for you." I thought he was joking. He wasn't. There I was with the largest roof in Cheshire on the ground and no way of getting it back up there. On top of that, the government inspector was due in a few weeks for a check up. Anyway, I dug in my heels and spent the next week making phone calls and pulling all the strings I could to find another company to put the roof back on for me. I eventually found someone and to no surprise, it cost me many thousands of pounds more. I never took the lowest price after that.

The whole project took about two years to complete and it was big success. Both Harry and I won awards from the U.K. Government for Housing and Design Excellence. I was so happy to receive my first award, and it truly meant the world to me. At that time, I did not really know the true value of that award, but years later, it would prove to be a real asset.

This development was also the first time I had also worked with another great advocate in my life named Phil Webster. Phil was a surveyor and had his own civil engineering company. They did all the groundwork, such as drains, concrete, foundations, etc. It was a very involved job, and you really needed someone who knew his or her stuff to get it right. If you screw up the foundations, nothing good can happen. Phil did a lot more than simply put in the foundations; he was a mentor to me. We would spend hours in the site cabin, and he would teach me how to schedule works and plan the weeks and months ahead.

I'm not sure why he did that for me. All I know is that I respected Phil deeply and truly enjoyed working with him. He inadvertently became a mentor to me and wanted to share his knowledge. We worked on many projects together over the next fifteen years and became great friends. I was always so grateful for his kindness and his willingness to teach me his skills without wanting anything in return. We lost touch for a little while when I moved to the USA but have tried to maintain contact over the years. In December 2013, we had planned to meet up when I was back in Manchester for a couple of days. Something came up and I texted Phil and told him I could not make it. He replied that was no problem, and that the next time I was in town, we would get together. I returned to Phoenix and thought nothing of it. About six months later, I received a message telling me Phil had died from a heart attack while riding his bike on holiday in Europe. My heart just sank, I wish I had met up with him. I can't believe that he is gone. You showed me true friendship and selflessness Phil. Fifty-two is far too young to leave behind your wife and children.

Human doings, not enough time just being.

My career continued to prosper, and I was now building more and more exclusive developments with Harry and Phil as my mentors and co-collaborators. The projects became more adventurous and more challenging as I stretched my creative knowledge to the limit. Awards were coming in readily, and I remember one time when my brother Richard and I were up for the same prestigious housing award. Richard was also a developer but on a much larger scale than me.

I was always in awe of my brothers. They both went to Manchester Grammar School, which was the best school in the region and one that I was not smart enough to get into. They both went to university, which I was not deemed smart enough for either. My eldest brother always took the brunt of everything and by the time my parents could focus on me, they had mellowed somewhat. I have stated how my father was always my champion, but he was still tough on me. He always wanted me to try my best and never give up. He was very particular and wanted me to follow his way of life. The problem was that I was not brought up like him. His mother died when he was young, and his father was very strict with him. He was brought up with no money and had to struggle for everything.

I was fortunate enough to have a prosperous childhood due to my father's hard work, good fortune, and determination to succeed. This essence was passed down to my brothers and me. Every so often, he would pass us little notes of wisdom or *Golden Rules,* as he would call them. Due to my father's childhood poverty, he learned to save everything so all his notes were on old bits of paper or used envelopes. He still uses old envelopes to this day for his notes.

Golden Rule Number One: "Learn to say no." Not maybe or any other indecisive comment, but just plain N-O. I thought it was a simple rule that sounded easy. But anyone will tell you that saying no is tough. Over the years, I have learned that no is a very empowering word, which allows me to be honest.

Gold Rule Number Two: "Honesty is not the best policy; it's the only policy." This particular rule has guided me well throughout my life. It's not what you do in public that keeps you honest it's what you do in private that really makes the difference. I'm not pretending to be perfect but there have been a number of times in business and life when I could have been dishonest and no-one would have known, but I would have known and that is what really matters. There are many other rules and I have tried to live by them all my life. In fact, when my father was seventy-five, I made a book of all his Golden Rules and published it for the world to see. I encourage my children to live by those rules today.

"And the winner is....Charles Sidi from Planetree Properties!" stated the announcer. I could not believe it. My brother looked over at me with a big smile and said,

"Nice one. Charles, you deserve it." I was so pleased to have won that award, but not because I beat my brother, who got the Silver Award. The reason was that this award was special to me.

It was special because two years earlier, I had convinced Roger Stephenson to take on this project.

"Roger, this could be a great niche project for Stephenson Bell," I said, "There's an opportunity here to do something unique with these old buildings." It had been around twenty years since I had first met Roger as a young child, and now I was sitting across the table from him and working with a true master of Modernist design. The project involved taking an old Victorian building with a "postage stamp" size patch of land in between some old derelict garages. The site had been for sale for many years, and no one touched it. I saw a diamond in the rough. It was in a superb location, but no one seemed to have the vision for the property. I knew that this could be special. Roger realized that potential as well. I bought the site, which was dirt cheap because nobody wanted it. We created a unique home that turned out to be exquisite. The patch of land was now occupied with a new white modern structure with cedar paneling that bridged the gap between the old Victorian building and the garages. Inside we created a glass staircase with a suspended glass bridge that stretched across the landing to connect you to the multilevel private master suite. It was beautiful, and this was my first foray into the modernist world of architecture.

At the same time I was building this particular home, I was building myself a new home for my growing family. We had started to outgrow The Shires, and it was time to move. I trusted Harry to design us a new home from scratch on a piece of land that I had found. This was a new experience for me as I was so used to taking old buildings and making them come to life again. Once again, his design and my vision blended perfectly. The house was called The Brindles, and it had a curved section that connected the two wings of the house together. We moved into that house at the end of December 1999.

Chapter 8: Eureka

As Sarah navigates the twisting and bumpy stretch of road, it reminds me that life is full of twists and bumps.

The millennium was in full swing. No banks had collapsed and the world didn't stop due to it becoming two thousand years old, the Doomsday predictions came and went. A new world of innovation was upon us and it seemed as if there was a new vigor to businesses as the Internet began to sprout shoots that would soon change all our lives. Steve Jobs had just introduced the iPod, which would soon revolutionize the music industry. Mobile phones had become so small they could fit easily into your pocket and technology was racing forward, making our lives simpler. It just felt like everywhere I looked new products and ideas were abound.

On one cold February night in 2001, Sarah and I were faced with something new of our own.

"This is brilliant," I noted, "Every household in the world is going to want one of these." There were all sorts of items on the kitchen island. Sarah was busy cutting up plastic containers, and I was dismantling a handle from an old orange plastic jug.

"Lets put this on here!" I announced. We kept messing around and adding things. We worked furiously into the night while our two boys slept soundly in their new bedrooms, which Harry had designed for them.

Sarah had come up with an idea to place a container on top of a cereal box as our two young boys always seemed to rip the top off the cereal box or the box was always left open and the cereal would go stale.

"If we place this on top of the box, we can have a lid that you can pour the cereal out of" she said. I instantly jumped on the idea and started drawing sketches and cutting up bits of plastic to simulate the idea.

Little did anyone in our family know that Sarah and I were on the cusp of creating something that no one had seen before. I had been reading a great book by James Dyson some months earlier that explained his journey from invention to reality. He was the famed vacuum cleaner inventor and a number of other previous products that did not quite make it. The book explained his struggles, trials, and tribulations. I was definitely inspired by this great British industrial designer as we set to work.

Eureka!

By the morning, it was finished. We were both bleary eyed and not quite ready to do the morning duties required of young parents. I was so excited by this invention, and I had made a drawing to go with the model we had created out of plastic parts. As I had explained, this was the age of invention and Apple, for example, had brought out their new Apple desktop in a variety of cool colors that seemed to bring inanimate objects to life. These objects had begun to have a place in people's homes and innovative products took center stage. I visualized our invention in the same way. It would be designed from a clear blue plastic that was aesthetically pleasing with a sliding lid and handle. It would be modern and sleek, and there would be no more hiding those cereal boxes in the cupboard. Our invention could sit proudly on the counter in the kitchen.

Dyson explained in his book about how important it was to get protection as early as possible into the invention so I decided to contact my real estate attorney to make sure that I had someone verify the invention right away. . "Anne, it's Charles Sidi. Can I come and see you?" I asked hurriedly through the phone as I unlocked my car and proceeded to scrape the ice from my windshield.

"Of course, Charles. I will be free around 10:00 AM, what's it about?" she replied. "I'll explain when I get there, okay?" I said excitedly. It was now just after 9:00AM, so I set off in my car and headed to her office in Manchester. Sarah was just looking at me with a worried look on her face as I drove off with our new invention strapped in the front seat.

She had a sixth sense of what was to come but did not voice it. She almost wished she had never said anything to me that night. She knew that once I got an idea in my head there was no stopping me. I would choose my road and stick to it until the bitter end. As I drove my car on the motorway, I had already visualized the name of the product and could see it on all the shelves of every supermarket in Britain, if not the world. World domination—here I come.

I was still building at this time, and my brother Richard and I had been working on a residential development site together in Castlefield for the past year or so. Ironically the site was directly opposite to the old schoolhouse that Stephenson Bell had once occupied many years before. We launched the building just before September 11th, 2001. As you can imagine, it was not the best time to launch a brand new multi-million pound development.

The cereal box topper, which I called EasiPour, had also taken on a life of its own. While developing the project in Castlefield, I had spent many hours drawing and refining the design. Dyson had made hundreds of models of his inventions to perfect the design. I was so inspired by this that I decided to do the same. My first task was to buy the most popular size of cereal box. Of course, this was the famous Kellogg's Cornflakes. At that time, I had rented a small office in an old Victorian building not too far from my home. The owners of the building were a father and son called Keith and Robert Leggett. Robert had recently started a new recruitment company in the IT world. They occupied a couple offices, and I had a small space of about 100 sq. ft on the ground floor.

Over time we became friendly, and Robert and I would talk about my invention and my real estate business. I liked Robert from the start. Like myself, he was very entrepreneurial and not afraid to take risks. I think he thought I was a bit mad, but he appreciated my spirit.

Over the next few months, I could be seen coming into my office carrying numerous boxes of cereal under my arm. I think Robert's staff just thought I liked Cornflakes, a lot. I would spend hours making models out of cardboard, which were perfect and the lid would slide back and forth as I had envisioned some months before. I would number and date each model and mark it with my patent pending number. I had engaged a patent attorney and the long laborious process of patenting had also begun.

After making all the models, I had reached a point where I could go no further on my own and started to seek out an industrial product design company that could help me take it to the next level. I was so used to working with different companies on my building projects; it was just like engaging an architect. A friend recommended a company that had invented and developed products for the dental industry, owned by a man named Alan Segal. The first time I met Alan, he was shocked and surprised at my approach. He had never met anyone that had come so prepared. Prior to the meeting, he had explained to me that he did not really engage in outside work. His company only developed and created their own products. I explained to him that he would not be wasting his time, and it was imperative that he meet with me. My passion was clearly too much for him to resist.

I arrived at his office with a box full of my cardboard 'prototypes' of EasiPour. I had developed a brochure to explain the use of the product, how I would sell the product, and its distribution to the market. I also had a non-disclosure agreement for him to sign in accordance with my pending patent.

"Wow," he said, "you really have got this together." I sat back in my chair, trying to look cool and said

"Thank you, can you help me?" We talked for a couple of hours and by the end of the meeting, we had an agreement. They would take my designs and produce 3-D drawings, as well as actual working models. This was it—world domination. I was only thirty years old, and I was ready to make it big.

Everyone remembers where he or she was when the twin towers were hit, and I was no exception. We had just completed the final engineering drawings for our invention, EasiPour. I was at Alan's office, and he was frantically talking on the phone to some of his business colleagues in New York. He had a television in office, which I thought was very state-of-the art, and all I could see was the image of this plane smashing into one of the towers. I quickly picked up my mobile phone and dialed Sarah. It was about 3:30 PM in the afternoon, and she was picking up Adam and Joshua from their school and nursery. Since it was September Adam would be coming out of school wearing his "long trousers". Yes, Adam went to Altrincham Preparatory School and Joshua soon followed.

"Have you heard?" I said with a quiver in my voice, "A plane has hit the World Trade Center in New York!" She had heard and was as dumfounded and frightened as I was. My meeting was abandoned, and I rushed home. Like most people all over the world, we spent the coming weeks glued to our television sets. I honestly thought we were going to witness World War Three. I never really understood what an impact this had on me until sometime later. About a month after the attacks, Joshua, who was two, came home from his nursery school with a drawing he had done. It was an image of the two towers falling to the ground with people jumping from the windows. I had not even realized that he had absorbed all this information. It was a constant reminder that we are not in control of our lives.

We are mere co-pilots.

Chapter 9: Head Down, Chin Up!

If you actually try to do what the title of this chapter says, it's impossible. Go on, try it. Hopefully, you are all now trying to put your head down and lift your chin up. See, impossible.

Well, that's what I did for the next three years. I decided to take a sabbatical from the building industry after the development in Castlefield was completed, which both Richard and I won the award for "Best City Development." I pursued EasiPour with all my heart and soul. I kept my head down and tried to keep my chin up at all times. The seemingly easy process of bringing a brand new idea to market with zero experience was proving to be almost impossible.

I didn't care; I had my rose colored glasses on, and my passion for the product just took over. I literally ate, slept and breathed that product for the next three years. I was determined to make it a success. Little did I know that nine years later, keeping my head down would play another significant part in my life.

"Charles, keep your head to one side," Sarah warns.
"Sorry, but my neck is killing me," I say abruptly.

"I thought you were going to talk to me to keep me alert. I have not heard a word from you for the past hour," she continues, "Are you okay?" I am just holding it together and trying not to think about what the future may hold.

If you have ever driven from San Diego to Phoenix, you will know that it is a very boring drive with very little scenery and just large patches of desert. We had made this journey in the month of July for the past five years, as we would leave the summer Arizona heat for the cool ocean breeze of California. It was like an exodus from Phoenix. All our friends would travel there, and we would spend the whole month enjoying the cooler weather, while the boys would learn to surf and skateboard on the boardwalks. I would spend some of the day working and the rest enjoying time with my family. As everyone else left for the summer, I actually did more business and made more connections on the coast of California than I would ever have done if I stayed in Phoenix. In fact, I met my business partner, Rick, in California.

"I'm terrified. I have already been through so many surgeries on my eyes and now this has happened." The sun is coming up. I take a look at my watch and it is just after 5:00 AM. It is beautiful, and the sky starts to change from dark blue to a color resembling indigo with a tinge of orange. Sunrises and sunsets are spectacular in the desert. Will I ever see one again? "I know I'm going to have to have my head down again for the next week," I say. Sarah just nods. The last time I had to do this was the first time my retina detached in the left eye.

I had recently turned thirty-eight, and it was just before Passover. We had been in the United States for only a year and a half. I had been struggling with my vision for sometime and saw a quack doctor who told me everything was fine and that my symptoms were nothing to be worried about. She had scanned my retina and told me everything was in place. Fuck, hindsight is truly a wonderful thing. If I knew what I know now, I would have seen an ophthalmologist right away!

Unfortunately for me, I had gone to see an optometrist who was no good at her job. In the U.S.A., I did not know there was a difference between an optometrist and an ophthalmologist. Well, it turns out to be another another ten years of training, that's all.

"The retina is fine, Charles," the optometrist said, "I really don't know why you are having all these symptoms." I trusted her and went home. My symptoms seemed to get worse, which was a flood of floaters. That's the vitreous in the eye pulling away from the retina and flashing lights. It seems obvious now, but the retina was literally pulling away. The next thing I knew, my vision was becoming weird, and I could not see very well at the top of my field of view. This was the retina falling down into my macular vision. How the fuck could she not have seen that?

The next day, I went to see my general doctor and he sent me to see an ophthalmologist—you know, the one with all the training.

I was in there for three minutes, and he looked into my eye, sat back in his chair, and proclaimed, "You need surgery right now!" Boom! Those words hit me like a train. I thought everything was fine because the other doctor had been telling me for months that there was nothing to worry about. I was extremely distraught.

In that moment, my life changed. It was 3:00 PM on a Wednesday afternoon. Sarah was picking up the boys from school. I called her. "Sarah, it's me. I need surgery right away; my retina has detached!" I told my wife in a panic stricken voice. The phone was silent for a moment as she registered what I had just told her.

"I'm coming now. I'm on my way."

From that point on, it was complete mayhem. I was sent by the ophthalmologist to see a retinal surgeon. Her offices were down in a part of Phoenix where I had never been to before. We lived in Scottsdale at the time, and certain parts of Phoenix were quite alien to us.

Sarah had picked me up, and I was in the passenger seat, shaking and crying. I could not believe it. This was bloody serious. I had absolutely no knowledge of what was about to happen to me. My usual eye exam consisted of an eye test and not much more.

We arrived at this dark office with lots of people in the waiting room, with an average age of ninety.

Most of them had eye patches on and were sitting with their heads down. I didn't take much notice. We waited in line and then proceeded to sit down. In the corner of the room was a television showing some old movie. No one was watching it, and all I could think was why would they have a television in a doctor's office for people who can't bloody see! The noise of the television was irritating me, and I just sat there with my head in my hands. Fortunately, a few minutes later, a technician called out and said, "Charles Seedee." I stood up and we followed her down a narrow corridor with lots of doctors walking around. She led me into a small room that was about 8 ft. by 8 ft. In front of me was a black mechanical chair with the eye exam equipment close by.

The technician had already seen my notes from the ophthalmologist; I'm guessing they sent them over electronically. I was impressed. Once she had finished her triage, a doctor came in. It was a woman with what seemed to be a strong German accent. I will never forget what happened next. She lay me down in the chair and then proceeded to put this contraption on her head and picked up a thin metal tool, which looked like something you would see at a dentist's office, but not sharp. The lights went out, and all I could see was this super bright light beaming from her head. My eyes had already been dilated so my iris was now as big as my eye! The light actually hurt my eye, and I wanted to constantly sneeze. As you can imagine, sneezing with a detached retina is not the best thing to do.

She asked me to look left, right, up, and down while she poked my eyeball with the thin metal tool. I was in such a state of shock that I just froze. The exam was finally over and I was completely blinded as she started to talk to me. "If we don't do surgery right away, we are going to have to remove your eye." Oh my Lord, I wanted to throw up. The room was spinning and my head was banging.

"Sorry, what did you say?!" I must have heard this wrong. She repeated it verbatim!

She obviously had no bedside manner whatsoever, and I was now feeling really scared. Take my fucking eye out! That's all I could hear in my head over and over. The place was freezing, as the air-conditioning must have been on thirty degrees below zero. Sarah was sitting in the side chair. She was so cold and frightened that we just did not know what to do. It was all going way too fast.

Before I could say another word, another doctor came in and although he had a better approach, he did the same exam she did. Why they had to do that, I don't know? It was fucking torture. "I can do the surgery on Friday," he asserted. But the female doctor just informed me that if I did not get surgery right away, they might have to remove my eye!

"No, no!" I blurted out, "she said I need it right now." They both left the room. Sarah and I just stared at each other not saying a single word. I just wanted to go back to Manchester, to go home. I felt so alone. It was just like that first day at boarding school, I just wanted to go home and be safe. There is nothing worse than being ill in another country. The system was different here, and everything was new. I had no barometer to gage the quality of treatment. We had only been in the USA for a relatively short time. We had made some friends, but they did not really know us all that well. We were all alone in that small freezing room. We only had each other.

Dig deep, I thought. Pull it together, man! I know you can get through this. C'mon, Charles, dig deep. I started to pray in my head. Polacks had taught me to draw upon my religion and my faith. I was not really a very religious person, but I was always spiritual. I had been putting on Tefillin for the past year or so as my Rabbi had suggested that I might enjoy it. He was right. I did and still do. Each day, I wrap the leather around my arm seven times while saying the

Shema[16]. It keeps me honest. It's like looking in the mirror and telling yourself to be a good and decent person and try and go through the day with positivity and gratefulness. I drew strength from this.

The door suddenly opened once again and the lady with the German accent came in. "Okay, Dr. Gordon will do surgery tomorrow." I had no idea who he was or if he was any good. I was now in his hands, quite literally. That was it. I was told to come to the surgery center the next morning at 8:00AM and not to eat or drink after midnight. We got back into the car and drove home. I was a complete wreck, and I could not quite grasp what had just happened. I was now facing major eye surgery to save my eye. It had all gone from zero to sixty in milliseconds!

I met Dr. Gordon for the first time just prior to the surgery the next morning. I could not see his face properly as my eye was already dilated and ready for surgery. They must have administered a hundred drops. "My name is Dr. Gordon," he said calmly, "nice to meet you; everything is going to be fine." We talked for a few minutes and then, he was gone.

I remember thinking he seemed all right, and the nurses had told me he was the best. Perhaps my silent prayer the day before in that freezing consulting room had worked?

I was then wheeled into the operating room, awake! They had given me a facial block so I could not feel anything, and I could hear music playing in the background. I saw the large operating light, which was incredibly bright with lots of people milling around. "We're going to give you a drug that will make you sleepy, Charles, but you will be sort of awake because we need for you to be able to respond to our instructions during the surgery," one of the nurses said. "Okay?" I murmured quite nervously. Wow, I thought. This is going to be weird. It was.

---

[16] Jewish daily prayer

I could hear the music, and it felt like I could feel them cut my eye off, a bit like taking the top off a boiled egg. Suddenly, it was like looking through a kaleidoscope. The colors were amazing, and I could hear the doctor talking from time to time to his staff as I drifted in and out of consciousness. Every so often, I would feel the blood pressure monitor grip my arm for a while and then relax as the pressure was released. This seemed to go on and on for hours. "Charles, stay very still," I heard Dr. Gordon say, "hold your breath and breath out." I just did as I was told and drifted off again. This happened a number of times. My arm would tighten up with the grip of the monitor and bring me out of my dreamy state and then I would hear the same instructions.

Apparently I was in there for six hours as Dr. Gordon tried to repair my eye. It was a tough surgery. Thank goodness they did not take out my eye as the German doctor had told me.

"Charles, it's Sarah." I felt her warm touch on my arm. It felt so good to hear her voice. It was over.

I went home that night with some pain relief and Sarah as my nurse! After a very uncomfortable night and feeling like someone had put an axe in my head, I retuned to the doctor's office in Phoenix the next morning.

There I was, with my eye patch on and my head down, trying to keep my chin up!

My Father David Sidi (1975)

Polacks House Clifton College

Clifton Suspension Bridge, Clifton Bristol. (if you look closely you can see
the railway line exiting the dreaded tunnel during our 'Night Op"

74

My Grandfather Jack Rubin with his winning horse at the Grand National

Charles and Sarah.
Sarah's 20th Birthday 1994.
One week after our first date.

Our wedding day August 27th 1995.

The Shires
The first house I built at age 19.

Gawsworth New Hall Barn, "the biggest roof in Cheshire."

Winner of Housing Project Award from the UK Government 1996.

Stephenson Bell House- Winner of the Best of British Homes Award 2006. With my award below

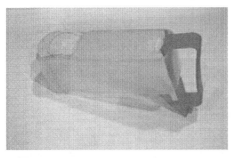

Cereal Topper that we made
in our Kitchen. 2001

Packaging for the Kellogg's EasiPour

The Kellogg's EasiPour by
Sidi Products Ltd.
This was the cover of our
marketing brochure.

Just off the plane -arriving in the USA, Dec 15th 2006

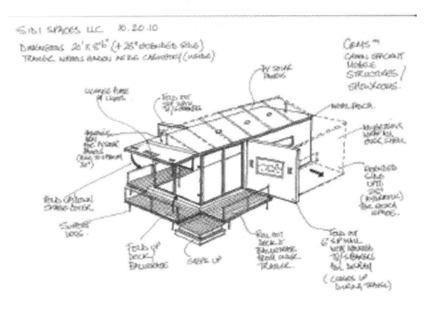

**Napkin Sketch of the BizBox- which was called GEMS
originally, October 2010 Dec 15th 2006**

Me with the very first BizBox.
Photos taken during our film shoot. June 2011

Chapter 10: Climbing A Mountain

It's not until you have slid all the way down the mountain that you realize how long and arduous it was to climb it.

EasiPour was my mountain, and I had my boots strapped on, ready to climb over any obstacle that got in my way. However, before climbing any mountain, it's important to have the right equipment and expertise. I had neither, apart from pure grit and determination. You also need to recognize when blind faith is not enough. You need to know when to stop.

I had now shown my product or idea to a few friends and family, all of whom thought it was brilliant. No one said, "That's shit, Charles," or "I'm not sure if that will work." They all said it was great. That was just pouring fuel on a fire.

"Stuart, its Charles Sidi. How are you doing?" I began eagerly.

"Charles, it's great to hear from you. How's the family?" he replied.

"Doing great, thanks. Adam is now five and is attending APS[17]. and Joshua is two. " Stuart was a long time family friend who also attended APS as a child and without a doubt, an entrepreneur and

---

[17] Altrincham Preparatory School

brilliant business man. He was only a few years older than me but already had significant success in his business life. I liked Stuart, and I knew that he had worked with Kellogg's in his previous business. He was the perfect person to get some advice on EasiPour.

"Can I come and see you? I have an idea for a great product that I think will work perfectly for Kellogg's," I told him. He was intrigued, and we arranged to meet later that week. Stuart, similar to the other people I had shown EasiPour to loved it. This was a significant step forward in climbing my mountain. Stuart had a lot of connections at Kellogg's, and he thought they would be interested in EasiPour.

Before I knew it, Stuart had set up a meeting with Kellogg's. The Kellogg Company, although headquartered in America, had their main UK office in Manchester. Yes, Manchester. They were only about twenty miles away from my home. It was all coming together. I was thinking that this was going to be easy. Stuart and I arrived at their head office, and I was dumfounded. It was huge with a large glass atrium with all the offices based around the atrium.

"We're here to see David," Stuart said calmly. I was shaking inside and trying to act cool at the same time. They asked us to sign the visitors' book and then handed us Kellogg's guest passes. This was a totally new experience for me. Stuart was not fazed by any of it. He had been to this office many times. I was in good hands.

We waited in the large atrium watching old Kellogg's television ads on the monitor. We were surrounded by all the Kellogg's characters that adorned the walls—Tony the Tiger; Snap, Crackle, and Pop; and of course, the Corn Flakes Cockerel. I was pretty intimidated by all of this but just took a breather and told myself to be confident and believe in myself.

You have to note that I did not have a product yet, only an idea. I simply had my homemade plastic model and my drawing. I can't actually believe that we went in to that meeting with nothing. Anyway, Stuart believed it was enough, which was fine with me.

"Follow me," the young lady said to us as we sipped our coffee. She guided us to a large glass elevator and hit the 4th floor button. Stuart made general chitchat as one does in an elevator as I looked out at the atrium below. Then, the door opened with a ding. We were guided down a long corridor, passing many cubicles with lots of people working furiously. I noticed drawings of the Kellogg's characters on the desks with what looked to be new advertising campaigns and promotions. I was excited.

We arrived at David's corner office. David and Stuart had known each other for a number of years so they hit it off and were catching up. I just sat there in a daze trying to stay engaged.

"Charles, show David your idea," said Stuart. I was a little startled as I fumbled in my briefcase to reveal what I had created. Even though I was nervous, you would not have known it. I've always seemed to have an ability to hide that kind of thing in stressful situations.

"Here you go," I said, "it's called EasiPour." I could see David trying to not let his eyes light up, but they did. That was enough for me and my confidence grew. We spent about half an hour with him explaining what the product would do and how we thought it would be a great product for Kellogg's. He liked it, and he said would like to see more as we developed it.

Both Stuart and I were excited as we handed in our guest passes and headed to the car park. About a week later, Stuart was my first investor. I set up a new company called Sidi Products Limited. And with my new investment for stock, I was able to develop the product. Stuart was another advocate in my life and believed in my vision while being a true gent from start to finish. Soon after, other investors followed, and I had now had a real company. I took the responsibility of the investment very seriously as this was people's hard earned money. I would not let them down.

About six months had passed, and I was still working out of my 100 sq. ft office that I rented from Rob and his father. I felt as if I needed to get some help and expand a little. There was a lot to do,

83

and I was not able to cope on my own. I employed a secretary who was in her sixties that Rob had recommended to me, and I moved into a larger office on the second floor. By now, I had started work on the engineering of the product with Alan and his team, and we were close to seeing our first real working prototype. Rob was excited by my progress, and from time to time, I would keep him updated. His company had started to grow significantly and now had about ten people working out of a small office. I admired his tenacity and vision. We were both young and ready to take on the world.

It was not long after I had moved into the new office that I received a call from Kellogg's. "Charles, its Richard from Kellogg's." Richard was Head of Licensing of Kellogg's U.K. and worked directly with David. I had been working with him for the last six months on how to bring the product to market. I desperately wanted to have Kellogg's brand on my product, so it would be called Kellogg's EasiPour. Not an easy task, I can assure you.

"I want you to speak with my boss in America about EasiPour. I would like her to see it," he said casually, "Can you fly out to her in Battle Creek, Michigan, and show her the product?" I stopped and thought about that for a moment. He wanted ME to go and see his boss in America!

His boss was Head of Worldwide Licensing for Kellogg's. I can remember that phone call to this day. I was actually on the way back to my office from picking up a sandwich for lunch when my mobile rang. *My heart was racing as he asked me to see if I could go to their global headquarters and see his boss. Of course I could go.*

"Of course Richard, but I'll have to check my diary (calendar) to see when I can go," I told him confidently. There was a pause and I thought *shit!* I should not have said that.

"Ok," he said, "just let me know when, and I will set it up."

I just sat down on the floor outside the office and laughed my head off. There I was, working out of a little 200 sq. ft. office with my secretary, and Kellogg's had just invited me—yes, me—Charles

Sidi to fly out to their world fucking headquarters in Michigan. At that moment, I felt as if all the hard work I had done for the last year was beginning to pay off. It was a surreal feeling. I picked myself up and waltzed into my office with the biggest smile on my face. World domination, world domination!

About a month later I was on the plane with my secretary. Ridiculous, I know. I did not need to take my secretary, but I thought it would look good. Fake it until you make it, right? We arrived in Chicago and the whole way, I was thinking to myself, I've made it. This is going to be huge. If I get a worldwide licensing deal, it will be insane. Fortunately, I actually had our first working prototype, and it was perfect. The product did exactly what it said it would do and Kellogg's UK loved it. I still had no deal with them, but I knew in my heart and soul that I would get one.

We drove from Chicago to Battle Creek, Michigan, and made good time not to be late for my meeting. The offices were immense, and I mean gargantuan. I thought their office in Manchester was enormous; this was like a city of its own. I asked my secretary to wait for me while I went to the bathroom. I looked at myself in the mirror and remember saying to myself, "Don't fuck this up, you can do it!" I straightened my hair and pinched my tie high up into my collar and strutted out in readiness for the meeting that soon followed. After the usual elevator ride and long walk to the meeting room, Richard's boss confronted me.

She was a small lady but very neatly dressed with a strong accent. I liked her from the start. She was tough, a real firecracker. This woman had probably one of the most important jobs at Kellogg's, worth billions of dollars. "So Charles, or is it Chuck?" she asked.

"It's Charles," I replied in my English accent, which I think she liked. My secretary was sitting at the large boardroom table ready to take notes. It was almost comical. I kept a straight face. I took out the product and proceeded to show her how it worked and why I thought it would be a win-win for all parties concerned.

"Richard has already shown me the designs, so I'm up to speed," she interjected, "let's discuss the license." I had already sent her a draft of the legal document that contained the license deal. She had that in front of her, but it was covered in red lines. I didn't really care about that; I just wanted to hear her say she would agree to a deal in principle, and we could work out the details over the coming months. We went back and forth for quite sometime about what she wanted and what I wanted, yet in the end, she looked at me and said, "I like it Chuck. I will let Richard know, and we can get a license deal in place." That was it.

I was jet lagged and exhausted from all the adrenaline rushing though my veins, and it honestly must have looked like I was on something. I remember actually pinching myself to check I was not dreaming. "Great!" I blurted out. The meeting was over and my secretary and I strolled out of the office and headed for the elevator.

This was huge! My product was now going to be called, Kellogg's EasiPour! My little company of just two people had managed to take on one of the largest companies and well-known brands in the world, and had them agree to put their prestigious brand on my product. It was indeed a victory that any entrepreneur would be proud of. I had just taken the product from ordinary to extraordinary.

As I write this now I can clearly remember how I felt and how funny the situation was. I do remember however not really celebrating the victories along the way. I just took it in my stride and thought that it was 'par for the course.' I am different these days, I recognize how important it is to really enjoy those moments of victory as they rarely come along and it's so easy just to 'chalk them up.' What's funny is that we spend way too much time worrying about all the bad stuff that happens along the way during our entrepreneurial journey and we forget to recognize the victories.

Chapter 11: All Or Nothing

"Kellogg's EasiPour, Keeps Freshness Locked in." That was our tagline. We had now moved out of the Victorian Building that Rob owned, which I think pleased him because he needed the space. His business was expanding rapidly. The IT world was growing quickly in the new millennium, and he had seen it coming.

I moved into a new office space of about 1500 sq. ft. with a new office manager and three large offices and a boardroom. Sarah had started to work for the company on a part time basis because we needed the help, and I employed her step-father Barry to help me drum up sales.

The licensing deal was done, and all I had to do now was sell them! Nevertheless, it took almost a year to get the licensing deal agreed with Kellogg's. It was like watching a cargo ship go down the Suez Canal. A little bit to the right, a little bit to left. Nothing moved fast. I had to learn to be very patient. The PR machine was winding up as well, so Sarah and I had already been featured in a number of magazines and newspapers about our invention and the licensing deal with Kellogg's.

As part of the deal, Kellogg's wanted us to do market research and focus groups to gauge a reaction to the product and whether or not there was a need. Looking back at this now, it was all just big corporate bullshit. Pardon me, but none of this was necessary. I just lapped it up though. I was young, and I was prepared to do anything to get the deal done. I had all my eggs in one basket. If they told me to jump, I asked how high?

It was a classic chicken and egg situation. We needed to make the product first and have it in production before we could sell any. I spent many months showing off the prototypes trying to gain orders from large companies, but the buyers wanted to see the real thing. We had to go all in, all or nothing.

We had found a local manufacturer to make the product for us from the "tools" we had engineered. I learned on the job, much like the time when I built my first house. I just pushed hard each day. The manufacturer had been making plastic injection-molded products for the music industry, which included mostly CD cases and some kitchen products. They had been in business for many years and were very experienced. The manufacturers loved EasiPour and thought it would be a great new line to their already very successful business.

It took about a year or so to get the product into production and during this time, I spent most of my days working with them on getting the product just right. I also had to make sure Kellogg's was happy with their logo that was now emblazoned on the product. I am sure we have all heard how excited entrepreneurs get when their product starts to be massed produced. I can tell you that this is a true feeling. There is something very special and exhilarating when you see your product come to life and it starts popping out of the huge metal tool that was fabricated to millimeter precision. I had worked tirelessly to get the idea to this day, and it was indeed amazing to see the product we had invented a year or so before with the Kellogg's brand on it. I did remember thinking, *"Shit, now I have to sell them!"*

Fortunately the manufacturer was happy to do a small run to allow me time to get orders, but that would soon change.

The first deal I did was with a very large kitchen product company called Lakeland Plastics. They are very well known in the UK and had an enormous mail order business for kitchen products. After a number of meetings, they agreed to sell my product, and it was given pride of place in their brochure with a full-page feature. This was quite a coup. We did sell some units, but it was slow. I think we did about a thousand or so in the first few months. I was trying to work out why the numbers were not that great. Upon reflection, I think it was the price and the product really needed to be demonstrated.

We proved this by doing a trade show in Birmingham called The Good Food Show. This was quite an undertaking. I set about designing our booth, which was made up of a huge wooden cereal bowl that we stood inside of and an enormous inflatable Kellogg's Cornflakes box with our EasiPour cereal topper on top. It was fantastic.

Barry, Sarah, and I stood in that cereal bowl for three days and we sold thousands. I was right; we needed to demonstrate the product. People loved it! For the next six months, we worked incredibly hard just to set up meetings with the buyers of the largest supermarket chains in the UK. I had everything in place, production was ready, the packaging was done and the product was gaining traction.

All I needed was a big order!

"Charles, Charles! What do you want to order?" Sarah asks me, "The lady is waiting."

"What? Sorry, oh yes, I'll have a chocolate milkshake and some fries," I reply.

"Chocolate milkshake, two fries and a black coffee please" Sarah requests through the intercom. We are at the McDonalds drive-thru in Yuma. "I really need this coffee," says Sarah as I suck down the chocolate milkshake into my empty stomach. I can feel the ice cold shake absorb into my gut. It feels great.

"How are you doing?" I ask Sarah. I continue, "We're almost halfway home."

"Not too bad, this coffee should help keep me to stay awake as you're not helping much. Every time I look over at you, you're either asleep or in some sort of daze," she tells me.

"Sorry just had a lot on my mind."

"Well I could do with some matchsticks to keep my eyes open!" she says. As we once again drive off heading towards Phoenix, I start to think about how I could have done with some matchsticks to stay awake during those long nights that I spent working trying to take EasiPour to market.

Chapter 12: Xavier

I have never forgotten this name nor will I. What I am about to tell you is incredible and shocking all at the same time. I almost don't want to give this person a chapter in my book but it warrants it.

"**B**arry!" I shouted at my father-in-law, "we've got it, I've managed to get us in to see the buyer at J. Sainsbury. They want to see us next Tuesday at their head office in London!" We were both so excited. This was my big moment. All the work I had put in came down to this moment. By pure coincidence, a friend of mine had also been trying to get me to see the head buyer at Tesco. Both Tesco and Sainsbury's were the largest supermarket chains in the UK. If I could get both of these to carry my product, I had hit the jackpot. It's also important to note that Kellogg's UK and USA were both watching sales and ready to take the product into the USA. There was a substantial amount riding on this.

We set up the meeting with the buyer at Sainsbury's and were getting everything ready when I got a phone call.

"Hi Charles, I've got you a meeting with the Tesco buyer whose name is Xavier," my friend said.

"Okay great. Do you think we could do it next Tuesday as I will be in London for another meeting, and it would be great to do it at the same time?" I did not mention that my other meeting was with their biggest competitor Sainsbury's.

"Leave it to me, I will get back to you shortly," he said.

As I put the phone down, I could not believe it. Two of the biggest supermarkets in the UK wanted to see the product. It was incredible. I had climbed this mountain, and I was exhausted but I felt that all this effort was not in vain. A few hours later, my mobile rang. "Charles, you are in at 4:00 PM with Xavier next Tuesday, good luck!" my friend expressed. I thanked him, put the phone down, and proceeded to hug Barry.

Tuesday came around fast, so we set off for London early in the morning to make sure we we had plenty of time. We strategized the whole journey and tried to not to get too excited, although it was difficult not to get ahead of ourselves. You must remember that this was just our first meeting with them.

Our first meeting was with the buyer at Sainsbury's. Their offices were very impressive, but after having been to the Kellogg's HQ in the US, I was over all that big corporate headquarters stuff. I just took it all in my stride. I waltzed in and gave our names to the lady on the desk. I was an old hat at this stuff now.

We sat and waited for about forty minutes, which irritated me. I hate waiting around for scheduled meetings. We had travelled two hundred miles, and they couldn't be ready. It just pissed me off. Anyway, I was clearly the small fish, and they could do whatever they wanted I suppose. Over the years, I have always vowed that I will never let someone wait for a scheduled meeting with me. I just think it's rude and unnecessary. Eventually Barry and I were invited into this small office and the young buyer was sitting in there. I remember thinking, *bloody hell, this kid's young.* I was only thirty-one, so he must have been really young. I can't remember his name, and that's probably because he did not make much of an impact upon me, certainly not as much as Xavier did later that day.

We did the usual chitchat and then got down to business. I have to be honest; this was the easiest deal I have ever done. I am not sure why, it was like all the stars were aligned. He loved the product and agreed to stock it with a first order of 100,000 units! We agreed on the wholesale price and that was pretty much it. I looked at Barry, and he had his mouth wide-open ready to catch flies. We were both dumbfounded. We left that office on cloud fucking nine. "Oh shit! We fucking did it! 100,000 units just like that!" I screamed as we got in the car. We felt like kings. It was quite an unbelievable feeling. I had so many thoughts going through my head all at once. I was really on my way to making this a huge success. One of the biggest supermarkets in the country had given me a ridiculous initial order, nothing could stop me now!

We headed out of London and over to Tesco's head office that was about an hour away. Our heads were spinning, and we just could not stop smiling and laughing. We were so confident and cocky and strategized about our meeting with Tesco. I remember thinking to myself that if we can get both of these giants to sign up, the business would take off into the stratosphere. However life is not always that easy.

It was not long before we arrived at Tesco's head office, which was the complete antithesis of Sainsbury. It was a very nondescript building in an underwhelming industrial park. I did not care as I was so high from the Sainsbury deal, albeit I should have done. Tesco's business model was the opposite from Sainsbury's. They were all about lower priced goods for the masses, much like Walmart. Sainsbury on the other hand was more upmarket and sold to a higher income bracket demographic.

We signed in as usual and then were told to take the elevator to the third floor. Both of us had a spring in our step due to our recent victory at their biggest competitor. The elevator door opened, and we were confronted by a myriad of people working at their desks, all in one large space. There was no privacy at all.

I heard someone shout from over a desk in the corner of the room. "Are you the EasiPour people?" in what seemed like a French accent. We nodded, and he gestured to come over to his desk, but did not get up from it. Not even to shake our hands. Right then, I knew this was going to be tough.

He was Xavier, and he was the head buyer for food and ancillary products. He was huge, about 6'6" and 250 pounds. He was wearing a blue and white striped Rugby shirt and jeans, which is probably why I thought he looked like a rugby player. He motioned to us to sit down with his back turned to us as he typed on his keyboard. "Be with you in a minute," he said. This guy was arrogant. I looked at Barry, and we just sat there and said nothing. Yet both of us knew this was a bit strange.

"So, show me this EasiPour?" he questioned, rather rudely. Remember I had just been given a 100,000 unit order from Sainsbury so I was feeling very confident, too confident.

"Here you go" I said and started to demonstrate the product. He cut me off mid-speech and grabbed the product from my hands. "It looks okay," he said, "how much you asking?"

"One pound and ninety pence wholesale and you can sell at retail at just under four pounds," I replied. He just laughed right in my face.

"Bullshit, I will never sell it at that price!" Xavier laughed. By now, this guy was really beginning to piss me off. He was completely out of order to speak and treat us the way he had been doing. I kept my cool, but I was boiling up inside.

"I will give you ninety-nine pence for it." I knew I could not sell it for that as it almost cost that much for me to make it with the packaging and other components. I did not let that get in the way though. We were negotiating at least. Before I could give him a counter offer, he continued. "Oh and of course, you will need to pay us one hundred thousand pounds for the shelf space." I thought I had not heard him correctly and asked,

"Sorry, what did you say?"

"You know the drill. We need to be paid just to feature your product," he replied succinctly. Clearly, I did not know the drill. As they would say in the U.S., this was my first rodeo. I was so shocked by this and thought it was basic bribery. The next thing I said was not one of my better decisions.

"Well Xavier, we have just come from Sainsbury's and they have given a us a 100,000 unit order, and they did not ask for a shelving fee!" I was on a roll and continued, "And for that matter, they paid me one pound and ninety pence per unit." I wanted to continue and say, *"so and go fuck yourself!"* Fortunately I thought through that bit.

Well the next thing you know, he was out of his chair and threw the EasiPour right at me and reached across his desk towards my face with his big hands while screaming at the top of his French voice so everyone could hear. "Who the fuck do you think you are telling me what Sainsbury's has done. I don't give a fuck about them. I'm the fucking buyer for fucking Tesco!" I looked at Barry who was in shock, and I thought he was going to hit him. I could not believe what had just happened. I tried to calm him down but there was no stopping Xavier. He grabbed me by my suit jacket and literally picked me up out of my chair and threw my briefcase across the room. The room was now completely silent with everyone watching. It was so embarrassing.

He then proceeded to man handle me all the way to the elevator with Barry just following behind. "Get the fuck out of my office!" he screamed again. He was in a complete rage and his blood vessels were popping out of his forehead. I could also see in his eyes that he was enjoying every minute of it. He had all this power and was using it. This was like a nightmare but I was clearly awake! The madness didn't stop there. He came into the elevator with us, and we tried to reason with him. All I was doing was asking why we needed to pay a shelf fee. He did not care and continued to get annoyed with me. The elevator door opened and he saw us off the property. We had entered the world of Xavier!

As I reflect all these years later, I probably should not have said we had an order from his competitor, but I did have the right to question the outrageous shelving fee. It was completely unnecessary for him to treat us so terribly and get physical with me.

What really struck me was his arrogance. It's amazing how the corporate world works. Yes he was the buyer for Tesco, and I respected that but to abuse his power was misguided. Had he taken an idea from nothing and took all the risk of bringing it to market with shareholders and the weight of the world on his shoulders? No, of course not.

He had worked his way up the corporate ladder (and there's nothing wrong with that) but along the way, it had gone to his head. He thought he could treat anyone the way he wanted. Well I have learned along the way that an action causes a reaction, and you can't just go through life crapping on people. It will catch up with you.

I'm not sure what you're doing now, Xavier but you made for a hell of a story.

Chapter 13: Face The Music

The sun has come come up, and we stop at a gas station, as Sarah needed another break. It is 6:00 AM, and she has been driving for almost five hours since we left San Diego. As she gets out of the car to go to the convenience store and use the bathroom, I also get out and stretched my legs. I wonder if she will come back with a pack of cigarettes that she most desperately wanted some hours earlier. The warm Arizona sun feels good on my face as I raise my arms above my head. The gas station is completely empty apart from our car, and the roads are still quiet. It's Sunday morning so I presume people are still sleeping. I know that the next few days, weeks, and months are going to be very tough because I have been through this before with my previous eye. But, this time I might be without much vision at all. This is a very scary prospect, and I am not really sure how to handle it. What will it be like to have no vision? I have a manufacturing facility to run with employees and customer orders to fulfill. BizBox is in full swing, and I am now faced with being out of action for quite sometime.

"What will I do about the business?" I say to Sarah as we drove off.

"Stop worrying about your work for once in your life Charles!" she retorts angrily, "You always put your bloody work first, what is wrong with you?" She is right, of course. I do always put my work first. I am a workaholic and probably unbearable at times. "You could go blind and you're worrying about fucking work, unbelievable!" she continues to herself.

We start to approach Phoenix and will soon be home and then I know the reality will hit. This is not the fun drive with the two of us together like old times. This is serious and potentially life changing for all of us. I feel guilty about putting her and my boys in this position, even though I have no control over my situation. It is a genetic thing you see, not an accident or anything like that, that causes my eye issues. It just happened. My retinas obviously do not work as they should.

I think now is the time to get my head together and deal with whatever is going to happen and face the music with a strong mind. I am not going to let this beat me.

We arrive home and both go to bed to catch up on some sleep. We have been awake now for over thirty-six hours. I speak with Dr. Gordon's assistant, and we have an appointment set up for later that morning to see him. Surgery can't be done on a Sunday, but I am already booked in for the next day. Monday, July 15th. This is Sarah's birthday. Yes, she has to take me to eye surgery on her birthday. Not much of a birthday present, as you can imagine. This is just killing me. A few hours later, we are in the same office I went to all those years ago with my first eye troubles. Since the initial problem, I have been going there every three or four months for regular check ups so most of the staff knows me by my first name.

I am actually calm and quite relaxed at this point because there is no going back; I have to face the music and let him do his job.

"I can't believe this has happened, Charles," Dr. Gordon says. "Not to worry, I will get you fixed up," he assures me confidently, "I have you in first." After a fairly long consultation and examination with the head contraption and the thin metal tool, it is time to leave. I am so used to this by now compared to some of the other things I had to endure over the last few years. It was breeze. I remember the time

I was administered a drug called Avastin, which is injected directly into the back of the eye. It's mostly used for people with macular degeneration. Well, of course, lucky me had an allergic reaction to it, which is very rare. And I could not see out of the eye for about three weeks. To combat the reaction, I was given six further injections of steroids in the eye, one after the other!

Before I leave, Dr. Gordon says to me, "I think it is a good idea for you to patch both eyes up to keep them from moving around too much." Wow! I am going to find out pretty quickly what it is really like to have no sight.

He patches the eyes, and we head home so I can go to bed. As I drift off to sleep, I dream about another day that was pivotal in my life.

Chapter 14: Another Sunday

This was not the first Sunday I had to deal with some bad news. We had sent all the units to Sainbury's ready to launch in some of their stores. We had all the end of displays ready, and it was now up to the British public to do the rest. We had worked tirelessly for about four months to get this launch ready. It was no small undertaking from getting the product manufactured, to its packaging, and then artwork approval for all the Kellogg's characters. The distribution chain had to be running smoothly and we had to make sure everything arrived in stores across the country.

Sainsbury's was a well-oiled machine, and they had a great software system that allowed me to check up on sales in real time and also see what had sold over the past weeks. This was a great way for me to control our inventory and next production run. We had been paid for the 100,000 units and we re-invested some of that money into inventory, which was about another 30,000 units or so.

Later, as my business partner, Rick, has said to me on a number of occasions during our BizBox relationship. "You can't open an ice cream store without the ice cream, Charles."

We had been in the stores now for a few weeks and sales had been initially okay, but seemed a little light. I was very nervous and not sleeping too well. I decided to go into the office that Sunday and check the numbers for the past few days.

I logged onto the server and opened up my account expecting the numbers to have increased. They hadn't. They had actually gone down by about 40%. I just froze, and as I was looking at the screen, it felt like the world behind me disappeared. It was like, in a film, when the camera focuses on the person and zooms backwards. That's exactly what learning about the sales felt like. There was no one in the office, and I just looked around for a moment. I felt a rush come from within, and I vomited all over my desk. I knew right then, it was over. I had climbed this metaphorical mountain and, in a flash, I had slipped all the way down to the bottom.

I cleaned up my vomit, locked up the office and went home.

Chapter 15: It's Over

After three years and hundreds of thousands of pounds, I knew we had to stop. Grit and determination were not enough. Why would I stop just because some numbers were down? I had seen the writing on the wall for a little while, and I knew that to get the product to really move, I would have to do an in-store demonstration, which was no small feat.

I remembered back to the Good Food Show and how well we had done by demonstrating the product. To replicate this in hundreds of stores across the UK would have cost us millions, and I was certainly not going to risk any more money, certainly not from my investors.

So I took the decision to call a board meeting and stood in front of all my investors and explained the situation. Sometimes in life, you have to be strong enough to tell people news they don't want to hear. Telling good news is easy. I had kept my investors updated at all times, so it wasn't as if they were completely thrown off by the news. They were all intelligent and sophisticated investors who understood the risks but that did not matter to me. I felt terrible. We had a lot of money left in the bank and I explained that the company would not invest another penny in EasiPour. I would close down the business and sell off all the stock and assets, and it would be given back to the shareholders as per their stock holding. I could have easily continued along with the business and burnt the rest of the money, but that was not my style. I felt like I was the one who was responsible, and it was up to me to get back what I could for everyone else. I felt I had made the right choice.

Surprisingly, the investors were impressed by my decision and thought it very honorable. I presume they thought I was losing a lot more than them and that my dream was gone. In any event, it completely humbled me, and I have never forgotten how hard that time was. You hear all the time that it's the businesses that fail that you learn the most from. Well it is true. At the time I was just so depressed and could not see the woods from the trees. I had to start all over again.

I had been out of building for quite a while at this juncture and getting back into that would be a hard road. Whatever ego I possessed was crushed.

I clearly remember the day when I was selling off all the company's office furniture. It was an awful feeling. I had built up this little company and achieved so much. My product had been branded by one of the largest companies in the world, and we had sold it in one of the largest supermarkets in the country. Yet, at the end of the day, here was someone telling me they will give me ten pounds for my desk!

It was pure torture. It was like getting an injection of stress into your veins at every step.

It took about six months of agony to finally close everything down. I was just turning off "taps to stop the water" everyday. We sold the entire inventory to a wholesale company at half our cost and Sainsbury's sold their units eventually. It took me a long time to get over and even today, I still think, "what if" as I pour my CornFlakes every morning out of my EasiPour that sits proudly on my kitchen counter. It took me almost ten years to get over it.

It's important to recognize what mistakes you have made and why you've made them. I apply the lessons I learn from mine as I move forward. Never again will I put all my eggs in one basket, or be influenced by a large corporate company, however big they are, and hope that it is my winning ticket. I will LISTEN to the market and focus my efforts on adapting to what the marketplace wants.

Chapter 16: Starting Again

I was bruised and battered but not out. I got back into building as quickly as I could because I had a family to look after, and I decided to sell our home. We did not need such a big house, and the market was good, so I knew I would make a profit on it.

We sold the house and bought a much smaller home in one of my brother's developments. We had no mortgage so all the spare cash was available to invest in a real estate development. It was a humbling time.

Before I knew it, I was back in the saddle. Building was obviously in my blood, and I had forgotten how much I enjoyed it. About a year after EasiPour was over, I got a call from one of my original investors. He asked me if I would build a house for him. He had found a site and wanted to see if I could build it for him. I did not do custom building for clients. My business model consisted of speculative development and selling properties once they had been completed or part way through.

I cannot tell you how gratifying it was to have an investor that still had faith in me and now wanted to invest in my talents once again. This showed me that I had done the right thing a year ago by closing down EasiPour and working hard to get back as much money as I could for my investors. It felt like vindication.

I accepted the offer, and I engaged Roger Stephenson as the architect. Roger, seemed like a perfect fit for my client and him. During this time, I also bought a site for development that would entail a large contemporary office building, two residential flats, and a retail store. I employed Harry to work his magic once again. His practice had now grown considerably and he was one of the largest architectural practices in northwest England. Harry put his magical pencil to work and initiated the overall design but then handed the project over to one of his senior architects. It's amazing how things had changed from the days when we sat in the pub and sketched out ideas together. I did not mind, simply evolution.

So, I had two projects running side by side. Roger was working on the initial designs for my client, and Harry was working on my development. Time passed quickly and I was very busy once again. The pain of EasiPour was beginning to slowly dwindle as I focused on new challenges.

I was back to wearing boots and a hard hat as a daily outfit instead of a suit and tie. I was comfortable being on site, and I felt in control again. The Stephenson Bell house had now been approved and was already out of the ground. It was a very complex design with a dry moat and a concrete bridge that connected the garage to the main drive. It was a spectacular design that would have to be built with millimeter precision. Fortunately I had the "A Team" working for me. Phil Webster was once again my grounds man, and he really handled much of the very detailed engineering that had to be in place. I had an excellent crew of sub-contractors, so I felt that I was in good hands.

There were many days when I felt like I had gone backwards in my career. I wanted so badly to make EasiPour a worldwide success. It wasn't the money that I chased; it was the burning desire to grow a substantial business. It was not meant to be, and I had to deal with that. The excitement of growing a business was gone and the ups and downs of being an entrepreneur still carried heavily on my shoulders.

I was tired and worn out, but I had to carry on and work really hard to start to feel good about myself again.

Building two large developments at once was quite an undertaking, but I was used to hard work, so I just plowed on. The Stephenson Bell house was proving to be a very tough project because it had so many details and intricacies that I had to really focus all my efforts on it. I had a good site foreman on my commercial development, so I was able to let him take control of that project.

It took almost two years to complete the Stephenson Bell home and it was incredible. It was the most beautiful house I had ever built. It took its toll on me, and I was completely exhausted by the end of the project. I hardly saw my family during that time, and I remember it being a time of work, work, and more work. I did not falter. I kept my head down and ground it out. The end of the project left me feeling incredibly empty. I had just built this unbelievable home that was held in high regard by many. I did not care. I had no feelings of gratification. I was completely numb.

It was up for all sorts of different awards, and I just thought to myself, *who cares about bloody awards?* I had won enough of those and this was just another one. Awards don't pay the bills!

Much later, I would really understand why I had won those awards, but at that time, I couldn't care less.

Chapter 17: Crossroads

Feeling numb and empty after completing the Stephen Bell house and my commercial development, I was now at a crossroads. What was the next step for me? Where have I come from and where was I going?

My father always taught me that indecision is the worst position to be in. I had come to a stage in my life and business career where I felt I had reached a saturation point. I still lived in the same town I was born in and lived in a small community where every one knew each other. I felt claustrophobic and was yearning for something new.

I think I am either an adrenaline junkie or someone is who not scared to just go for it. I would like to think I'm the latter but to be honest, the thought of creating something or doing something new is also part of it.

It was the summer of 2006, and Sarah and I had been married for nearly eleven years. Like most lasting marriages, we were doing the same routine: going to work, having dinner, taking the kids to sports, and etc.

The burning desire to change and my relentless optimism was starting to surface again, and it would continue to grow inside of me. We had recently gone to see my parents at their second home in Scottsdale, Arizona. We had been going there every year for the past ten years or so at Passover. We enjoyed it each time, and I had begun to like the American way of life and their positive attitude. It was just a holiday and nothing more.

During that holiday, I discussed with Sarah whether we should move to America, maybe some place like San Francisco or San Diego. She just looked at me as if I was completely mad. She knew I was depressed and feeling down so she humored me a little.

Sorry, Sarah, but that chink of hope was enough for me to visualize us in America. I wanted to start again. I wanted to explore new things and places, and I most certainly wanted to get out the UK. I hated the weather, especially the consistent rain and grey skies. Those who live in the UK know exactly what I am talking about. It's just depressing. It was the night of Passover, and I was sitting in my father's office in his home in Scottsdale, and I said to him, "I want to move to America. I need a new challenge." To my surprise, he took it in his stride; although, he was finding what I had just said to him difficult to process.

Timing had never been my strongest suit. If I had an idea, I would just voice it. I have always been like that, and I still am. "Charles, we are about to start Passover, and you tell me you want to leave England and move to America!" he exclaimed. Before I could reply, the door bell rang.

Fortunately, for both of us, the guests arrived, and we couldn't continue our conversation any further. The next morning, however, was a different matter. Something strange happened next. My father, similar to the way he had done many times before, supported me and even had an idea of how to move to the U.S.

"I did not sleep all night thanks to you," he said with a smile on his face, "I've had a thought and it's just a thought so don't get carried away." He also knew that once I get a hold of something, I don't let go. "If you remember, I recently built the guest house here, and I think the builder might be interested in selling his company. Maybe, just maybe, that could be a way for you to come to Arizona and start a building business here?"

I could not believe what he was saying. I was completely surprised and delighted by his reaction. He continued, "I remember wanting to move to America when I was building in San Diego, when I was not much older than you are, but your mother did not want to leave her family, so it never ended up happening." By now, I knew in my mind that I would do everything in my power to see this through. I had reached my crossroads and knew which direction I was going.

West.

Chapter 18: A Giant Leap

A few weeks passed, and we were now back in the U.K. Sarah was not too happy with the prospect of moving to the U.S.A, but she understood that I was unhappy and wanted to support me. She knew in her heart that one day we would have to leave our hometown for new shores.

"It will be fantastic," I informed her, "trust me, it will be the best thing we ever do in our lives." Sarah just looked at me and asked,

"What about my family, my friends, our little village? I'm happy here." I knew it was a big deal, so I tried not to push her too hard, but I continued to plan our eventual move. I just felt we had to do it. I knew it was the best decision for my family.

During the next few months, I made several trips to Arizona to meet with the building company and put a deal together to buy the business. The process was very complex, as I needed to agree to a deal prior to applying for work visas. If I bought a company and employed more than two Americans, I would be able to apply for the E-2 Visa, which would allow to us to work and live in the U.S.A. for an initial period of two years. The visa could be renewed upon submission and approval of documents for a further five years. That was enough for me. If we could get the first visa, I would risk taking the family. If it didn't work out after two years, we would come back.

What I didn't think of was that if it did work, and we had invested our lives in the States and had to come home because of a visa issue.

On my second trip to Arizona, I agreed to a deal with the owner of the building company for a fair price and explained to him that I would maintain his staff and him going forward. We put our money into escrow, and I was now able to apply for my visa. The visa process was not only complex but also very expensive and stressful. As usual, I kept my eye on the goal and did not waver. I still had some reservations about moving my young family five thousand miles away so I consulted with my good friend Rob. I remember his advice to this day.

"Charles, don't hesitate! If you have an opportunity to make a big leap like that and aren't held back by any commitments, just go for it, I would!" He was right and I proceeded.

I spent the next few months working all day on my building projects, getting them finished, and tidying up my affairs while spending all night on the telephone with my U.S. attorney and building company. It was exhausting yet exhilarating at the same time. The months went by so quickly and before you know, it was time to go. It was December 15th, 2006.

It had only taken me six months from the initial thought of moving to actually leaving. Must be a record or something. A few weeks before, we had loaded up our furniture and belongings into a container. Then, it was time to leave the house. We had five suitcases, that was all. We locked up the front door for the final time. We were leaving the U.K. Adam was ten and Joshua was only seven, and they seemed to take it all in their stride. It's amazing how children adapt to new situations. They seem much better than adults at it.

I decided to rent out our home initially. This was just in case we all hated it and wanted to come home. If all went well, I would sell it after six months or so. Sarah and I agreed that we would do whatever it took to make it work and try and immerse ourselves into our new life in America.

The taxi arrived and we piled into the car. "Going on holiday? Somewhere nice?" the taxi driver asked.

"No, were emigrating to America," Sarah replied. That's when it hit me. We would not be coming back to live in England. It was a giant leap of faith.

Chapter 19: Grateful

I wake up in a cold sweat and my heart is racing. I'm blind. I can't see anything! Did the surgery not work? What happened? "Oh shit, Sarah! I can't see anything!" I shouted.

"It's okay, Charles, you're still wearing the eye patches from the night before." I completely forgot that I still have the eye patches on. "Oh thank goodness for that," as I rip the patches off, and my pounding heart starts to subside. In one way, I am relieved that I have not yet had the surgery, but in another way, I know it is coming. I look at Sarah and wish her a happy birthday. I think this is going to be one she wants to forget.

My father has travelled all the way from the U.K. to be with Sarah and I over the next week. I called my parents the night I found out and told them that I would need surgery and asked my father if he would come out. He is seventy-nine and not as fit as he used to be, but that did not seem to matter. He packed his briefcase and headed to the airport. By a stroke of luck, he was able to get on the first plane out. That must have been an awful journey for him but as a father, one he felt he had to make.

"Charles, how are doing this morning?" my father asks.

"I'm fine dad. It will all be okay." I'm not pretending or making it up. I feel calm and relaxed, and I am ready to get on with it. I am prepared mentally for whatever lies ahead. This is not my first rodeo. I know what is coming and I have to be strong. My business partner Rick has said to me during one of our many tough days at BizBox, "We are the leaders of our families and it's up to us to set an example and show them strength of character." This is one of those times and I will not let my family down.

I put on my tefillin, like I do every morning and find my inner strength and resolve. I am grateful for my life and what I have achieved. I do not ask for help. I never ask for help when I pray. I am just grateful for what I have. I am grateful for another beautiful day, another beautiful sunset and another day with my loving family. I am ready.

As I look in the mirror for what may be the last time, I remember that this is not the first time I had had to dig deep and find my true strength.

As I look back on that week, it was a very difficult time for my family and me. However, I was struck by a moment that my father and I shared. As a father, I understood the true meaning of it. During that week, my father came into my room and looked at me as I lay on the bed with my head down. I could see the despair on his face out of the corner of my eye. He grabbed my hand with his big soft hands and with a tear in his eye. He looked at me and said, "You'll be alright son. Trust me!"

Chapter 20: Didn't See That Coming

Even with a lot of experience and knowledge, it's not enough to see the road ahead.

I had been in Arizona for about six months, and it was time to actually take over my new company. I called it Scottsdale Arizona Custom Home Builders. Even though I knew how to build and had over twenty years of experience, building in the USA was completely different. I was lucky to have a great team behind me that had been working in the previous company for many years. They already had many great sub-contractors and a good reputation. This did make the transition much easier.

As part of my deal with the previous owner, I was supposed to take over the company with ongoing business but when it was time for me to take the reigns, they had nothing in the pipeline. I had to start from ground zero. They had a small office in Cave Creek, which is literally a small cowboy town, just north of Scottsdale. I decided to move the office to a new location in Scottsdale, which better fitted my vision for the company.

I worked tirelessly to drum up new business and put my name out into the market place. I was beginning to see that it was not going to be so easy. Looking back on this, I was crazy to think it was going to be easy! Why would I think that? I had just moved to a new country!

My first customer was a doctor from my children's school named Dr. Greg Sanders. I liked Greg from the start; he was a Canadian and an entrepreneur at heart. I am not sure why he decided to engage my company and me to remodel his home. I guess he just had a good feeling about me. I worked really hard, and we completed a superb job for him. He seemed to be impressed with my work ethic and business acumen. Greg and I became friends during that project, and it would soon turn out to be a friendship that would remain strong. I would approach him one day with an idea that would continue to intertwine our lives.

The jobs after that seemed to come in, and I started to get a flow of business. It was nearing the end of 2007, and I felt confident that I would make the move to America work. During this time, we also purchased a piece of land in a very prestigious golf resort called Desert Mountain. It was my intention to develop a very high-end custom home on a lot that had wonderful city views to the south and desert views to the north. I employed one of the top architects in Arizona to draw up the plans, and I was excited to realize my dream of being a developer in the USA.

In January of 2008, I was starting to have eye problems, and I found that I would have to sit in my office with the overhead light off to see my computer screen properly. I did not think much of it at the time and just carried on. This was just the start of my turbulent times. Soon, I would be faced with a major life-changing health issue, along with the beginning of an economic downturn. Imagine this: I had a new custom home building business that I had invested my new life into, an extensive speculative development in Desert Mountain, and I had recently agreed to buy another piece of land with two partners in Phoenix. I don't think anyone predicted what was coming and I was no exception.

A part of my application for my E2-Visa was to write a business plan for my newly acquired building company. The usual format was implemented, which included a SWOT[18] analysis. I remember writing down the usual categories for each area and when it came to threats I wrote down the following headings: outbreak of war, terrorism, economic and real estate collapse.

Little did I know that I would actually tick off each of those headings during what turned out to be the world's worst economic recession since the Great Depression.

---

[18] Acronym for Strengths, Weaknesses, Opportunities, and Threats

Chapter 21: Keep Buggering On!

Sir Winston Churchill was famous for saying, "Keep buggering on!" during times of hardship. It's a very British term, which means to never give up and just keep going. This was my life. I just kept buggering on!

It was now early 2009, and we were all starting to see the effects of what was known as the Great Recession. Work was becoming very tough and new construction jobs were getting a little thin on the ground. A lot of building companies had started to go bust, and I was somehow managing to stay in the game. I could not believe it. Not only had I essentially lost sight in my left eye, but my business was also struggling. The house in Desert Mountain was nearing completion, and we would soon be faced with trying to sell it. This was a very unstable time, and my sleep pattern was not good. I would wake up worrying about what each day would bring and what new problem would I have to face. It was like fighting fires each day. There was nothing fun about my day. The deal in Phoenix was also starting to get difficult as the market had changed, and even though we had achieved a very difficult re-zoning[19] of the property to build sixteen contemporary town homes, we did not wish to invest further monies

---

[19] Term used in property to gain a new zoning for a property

into the project. I was also here with my family on an E2-Visa[20] and that had just been renewed after an incredibly stressful journey back to the U.K. to get an extension from U.S Immigration. I soon realized that my life was not in my control, which did not rest easy in my mind at all. They could revoke or refuse to grant a further extension to my Visa at anytime and then, where would I be? We had been in the U.S.A. for three years, and we had invested our lives there. We sold the house in the U.K., and there was no going back. I was not prepared to let my life be in someone else's hands.

In the true style of Sir Winston Churchill, I would find a solution and not stop until I was done. I just kept buggering on!

---

[20] Business Visa given to Non-US citizens

Chapter 22: Alien

I'm an alien I'm a legal alien
I'm an Englishman in New York
I'm an alien I'm a legal alien
I'm an Englishman in New York
By Sting

As I sit in the waiting room for my ensuing surgery, I am listening to one of my favorite songs on my headphones. It's amazing how music can take you back in time.

I had recently been staying with my cousin in Los Angeles and told him about my Visa situation. He explained to me that he was in the U.S.A. on a Green Card that allowed him to live in America indefinitely or apply for citizenship in due course. I was fascinated by this and asked how he came to get a Green Card. He explained that he applied under the "Alien of Extraordinary Ability." Due to his talents in the music industry, he had been able to get a Green Card through this route. He gave me the name of his attorney in Los Angeles and told me to call him, explaining that he would only take my case if he knew he would win.

That was all I needed—a slight glimmer of hope. I was on a mission. I did not realize that this route was only given to a few people each year. It was very specialized and difficult to achieve.

"Hi, my name is Charles Sidi. My cousin asked me to call you with regards to my Green Card application," I inquired over the phone.

"Yes, I was expecting your call, Charles. Simon told me a bit about you. Can you explain more?" he asked. I proceeded to tell him about all the awards I had won and the most recent, which was the Best of British Homes award for the Stephenson Bell house. As I was telling him about my achievements and awards, I started to realize why I had worked so hard for all those accolades. Would getting my Alien of Extraordinary Ability Green Card be a possible reward for all my hard work?

By the end of the call, the attorney informed me that he would take my case. He also told me to wire him $5,000 right away and that the remainder of the $5,000 was due on completion of the application. Of course, there was no refund!

I took a gamble with him, and he provided me with all the relevant paperwork and forms that I need to fill out. It took months for me to collate all the relevant information. I had to get verification of all my awards, and as you can imagine, it was not an easy task since some of them were from the British Government. I just plodded on and kept my eye on the goal. My life was in my control.

After many months, my application was ready to be sent to the U.S. Department of Immigration for processing. It was compiled of two large binder folders and a book I had written about my work and achievements. Nothing associated with the government moves fast, and I had already experienced this with my Visa process, so I knew to be patient.

After a year went by, I received a letter one day from the Department of Immigration. They had received my application, and it had been processed, but now they wanted more information!

I was taken aback. I had already sent them two large files of articles, magazine clippings, awards, and much more. It was a big letdown, and I really thought my application was in jeopardy. I spoke with my attorney, and he explained to me that immigration officers had become much tougher with this type of residency over the past year. He also explained that they normally didn't ask for more information, but he took this as a good sign because they normally just refused applications.

Great! I would have to start all over again. I went back further into my files and wrote to anyone that could help me. I wrote to the Head of Licensing at Kellogg's, and they wrote a great letter explaining my talents and abilities. I did the same with the Head of the Board for the British Homes Awards and the Minister of Housing at the British Government, who again both wrote outstanding letters. I had now compiled another file full of information and verification to my 'extraordinary ability' and was ready to send it back to the United States Department of Immigration for further processing. I was determined to get this done. I still felt uneasy about the situation because I was not sure it was enough.

One day, I was talking with a friend of mine who was attending a local talk and luncheon at The Rotary Club with Congressman Shaddegg. I honestly did not know much about him besides the fact he was my local Congressman, but what better person for me to talk to concerning my case? My friend told me the luncheon was in about an hour, and I could just turn up. I raced home from my office and changed into my suit. I grabbed some business cards and headed off to the luncheon.

I arrived at the golf club where the luncheon was being held and made my way to a table and sat down. I had been invited by my friend so it was not like I was crashing the party, although I would have done that if I had to!

There were the usual introductory speeches, and then Congressman Shaddegg got up and spoke for about an hour. It was very interesting, and one of his main topics was healthcare. It was around the time President Obama began discussions about a national healthcare system, which the Congressman was not in favor of. At the end of his talk, he asked for questions from the audience. I knew right then that this was my moment. I waited for a couple of questions to be answered, and then I stood up and took the microphone.

"Congressman Shaddegg, my name is Charles Sidi and I'm originally from the UK (as you can probably tell by my accent)" which drew some laughs. I was now on a roll. "Coming from the U.K., I have experienced a national healthcare system firsthand for many years. How do you expect America to adapt to a system like that?" That was all he needed to hear. He spoke for about twenty minutes in response to my question. He went on for so long that there was no more time for any other questions. I had the last one. He was certainly going to remember me.

After the talk was over I jumped out of my seat and ran straight over to him, introduced myself, and handed him my card. "Congressman Shadegg, great talk, my name is Char.." Before I could finish he said,

"Yes, Charles, great question." I knew I only had a few minutes, so I very precisely and clearly explained my immigration issue. He looked at me and said, "Here's my card. Call my office on Monday."

I was elated. That is what I needed to hear. I had the bit between my teeth and I was not going to let it go now.

Monday came around and I called his office and I was put through to his assistant. I provided him with all the relevant information, and he assured me he would look to try and help me. A few days later, I received this letter from his office.

Congress of the United States
House of Representatives
Washington D.C 20515-0304
April 23, 2009

Mr. Charles Sidi
8131 E Foothills Drive
Scottsdale Arizona 85255-4945

Dear Charles:

Thank you for contacting my office regarding the status of your pending I-140 application with the USCIS Nebraska Service Center. It was a pleasure meeting you at the Rotary Club Luncheon and hearing about your impressive talents and accomplishments in your field.

It is impressive to see the stellar recognition you have received from the British Homes Awards and the commendation credited to your work from the Minister of Housing and Planning in the British Parliament. It is my understanding that the British Homes Awards singles out the brightest, most imaginative, and innovative designs and I'm confident this was a true honor for you.

Given the recognition you have received in the United Kingdom, I am pleased that you have a desire to make Arizona your permanent home and continue to contribute your talent and expertise to our community.

Although as a member of Congress I have no direct day-to-day control over the U.S Citizenship and Immigration Service Nebraska Service Center, my office has contacted them and asked them that they review the impressive merits of your case. In the meantime, I encourage you to submit the additional documentation they have requested in your case in a timely manner.

As soon as we receive additional information, we will be in touch with you again. If you need further assistance please contact James Ashley in my Phoenix office.

Sincerely

John Shaddegg,
Congressman
Arizona 3rd District
U.S House of Representatives.

I did exactly as his letter advised and sent off the new information. Within three weeks of them receiving the new information I received a letter from the USA Immigration granting me and my family Green Card status under the status of Alien of Extraordinary Ability!

Looking back on this I think that you have to make your own luck. You can't let the world go by and think that it will all work out. I learned that you have to stay in tune with your surroundings, and keep your head up to watch out for opportunities that may arise. Those opportunities may seem insignificant at the time, but you never know until you try. I was not prepared to just sit back and let it happen on someone else's timeframe or agenda. As it happens, it is now five years since we received our Green Cards, and we have just applied for U.S. Citizenship and will be soon proud citizens.

JOHN SHADEGG
Third District, Arizona

WASHINGTON, DC OFFICE
436 Cannon House Office Building
Washington, DC 20515
(202) 225-3361
Fax (202) 225-3462

ARIZONA OFFICE
301 East Bethany Home Road
Suite C-203
Phoenix, AZ 85014
(602) 263-5300
Fax (602) 248-7733
http://johnshadegg.house.gov

Congress of the United States
House of Representatives
Washington, DC 20515–0304

ENERGY AND COMMERCE
SUBCOMMITTEES
ENERGY AND ENVIRONMENT
HEALTH
COMMUNICATIONS,
TECHNOLOGY AND THE INTERNET

SELECT COMMITTEE ON
ENERGY INDEPENDENCE AND
GLOBAL WARMING

REPUBLICAN STUDY COMMITTEE

April 23, 2009

Mr. Charles Sidi
8131 E Foothills Dr
Scottsdale, Arizona 85255-4945

Dear Charles:

Thank you for contacting my office regarding the status of your pending I-140 application with the USCIS Nebraska Service Center. It was a pleasure meeting you at the Rotary Club luncheon and hearing about your impressive talents and accomplishments in your field.

It is impressive to see the stellar recognition you have received from the British Homes Awards and the commendation credited to your work from the Minister for Housing and Planning in the British Parliament. It is my understanding that British Homes Awards singles out the brightest, most imaginative, and innovative designs and I'm confident this was a true honor for you.

Given the national recognition you have received in the United Kingdom, I am pleased that you have a desire to make Arizona your permanent home and continue to contribute your talent and expertise to our community.

Although as a Member of Congress I have no direct day-to-day control over the U.S. Citizenship and Immigration Service Nebraska Service Center, my office has contacted them and asked that they review the impressive merits of your case. In the meantime I encourage you to submit the additional documentation they have requested in your case in a timely manner.

As soon as we receive additional information, we will be in touch with you again. If you need further assistance please contact James Ashley in my Phoenix office at (602) 263-5300.

Sincerely,

John Shadegg
Congressman
Arizona 3rd District
U.S. House of Representatives

JBS:ja

Chapter 23: No Turning Back

I t is now 10:30 AM, and I am lying in the pre-op room as the nurses are going through their routine of numerous eye drops and setting up my facial block to numb the pain.

I know the drill. I am calm. I just lie there and think about my life and my family. Even though I do not know the outcome of the impending surgery, I have no choice. There is no turning back. Like many times before in my life, I have to move forward. I have to keep buggering on. It is just another crossroad, and I have to make a choice. I feel a sense of peace come over me, and I know that for whatever lies ahead of me, I will draw upon my inner strength and find a solution. I am good at that. I like to solve problems, and I have spent most of my life doing that. If I see a road block, I just plow right through it.

It's not before long I am wheeled into the operating room and once again see my now friend and surgeon Dr. Gordon. "It will be great, Charles, don't worry," he assured in his usual calm manner. I am not worried. I'm in great hands and I just want to get on with it.

I feel the nurse inject my arm as the solution merges with my blood stream, and I start to drift off.

Chapter 24: Out Of Adversity

Sometimes through adversity and a long journey, we can come up with something unexpected. The goal is to never stop discovering.

The economic downturn had really taken hold, and we were now well into the third year. It was late 2010, and I was becoming very frustrated with my situation. We had fortunately managed to sell the spec house in Desert Mountain and I won the award for "Best In American Living". I was very proud of that first American award. I had come to realize that winning awards had a much greater meaning than what people think.

The custom home building company had continued to bring in business, but it was certainly slower than the previous years. I was managing to survive the tough times. However, I could not see an end to the real estate downturn. The outlook was grim, and I recognized that it could be years before it would bounce back, if at all. The general mood in the country and the world was depression. It was time to keep your head down and do the best you could.

About a year earlier, I tried to drum up some new business and had taken courses on "Green Building" techniques as I always had an interest in this area of real estate. I needed something new with an edge in the real estate market, and this seemed like a good choice.

At the same time, I was looking to build an outside room or pool house at my home, and I explored the idea of a very quick build using insulated panels and lots of natural light. The space was no more than 400 sq. ft., and I thought it would be cool if I could design it so it could be built in a week or less. I created some designs and had my architect work on the plans. I was onto something, but I wasn't quite sure what I was onto.

I continued to explore the idea of quick green building techniques and set up a separate company called Sidi Spaces LLC. I thought I could run my innovative ideas through this company and keep it separate from my other custom home building company. I spent all my spare time working on those new ideas while working day-to-day on my custom home building projects.

Soon after, I was at a meeting with the Admissions Director at my son's new school called Tesseract, and he explained that they were growing and needed some new space. They also explained that they really liked green principles and the use of green materials. I could not believe it. Was it a coincidence or were my antennas just up?

"I have a great new 'green' building system and product that I think your school would be interested in," I told him. I did not really have too much work done on the concept, but this was all that I needed to spur me forward. I spent the next few days working on a presentation and sent it to him for his perusal. Within a day or so, the Head of School called me and said he would like to meet me and his Buildings and Grounds Committee to discuss my ideas.

I was delighted and set about preparing for my meeting. Once again, I had come up with something new and innovative that would hopefully help bolster my bottom line. The meeting went well, and they really liked the concept. I was then asked to flesh out the idea with the possibility of building a new annex to the school. I did not anticipate that the school would move slowly, although now, I'm not sure why I thought it would happen quickly. Many months went by, and I had started to develop a very concise green building system that would save time, money, and energy. I was not sure where any of this was heading, but I just kept moving forward, developing my system.

After a number of significant meetings with the School Board and almost a year of hard work, I was given the go ahead to design the new Middle School. I did not ask for a penny and I was happy to do the work gratis for the school with the outlook of gaining the building contract if it happened. We designed a magnificent scheme for the school based on my green building system. I was very proud of my design, and it had all stemmed from the pool house design I had done some years earlier.

Unfortunately, the scheme is still yet to be built. The economy hit really hard, and it is very difficult to raise money in times when things are so hard for people. I am sure that it will get built one day, and I will be very happy to see it go up.

I learned so much from the process, and it had given me something else to think about, something else to explore. As I have written many times in this book, sometimes you start something and you don't know where it will lead. This was just one of those times. As I had gained some traction with the green building system, I thought it would be a great idea if I could take my system on the road. I was not sure what that meant, but I did know that setting up a business in an industrial park and advertising heavily was not an option. But if I could design a building that I could take directly to my customer and let them see it in their own parking lot...now that was an interesting idea!

Chapter 25: A Simple Box!

I was sitting in my office one day, and I was thinking about my idea to take my green building on the road. I took out my sketchpad and started to scribble down some ideas, like you might see on a napkin. I knew what I wanted the building to look like. I started with the idea of a simple box and thought about how I could open up this box, much like a Pandora's box when it arrived at a customer location.

I was not concerned about the mobility; I was concerned only about the design of the box. This was first and foremost. Within an hour, I had drawn what I saw in my mind. It was October 10th, 2010. I dated the drawing and called it G.E.M.S. which stood for Green Efficient Mobile Structures or Showrooms. The box had solar panels on the roof, solar tube skylights, fold out walls, and lots of natural light via glass doors and a slide out portion to expand the space.

It was a light bulb flashing above my head moment. I had experienced this before. Yet this time, there was no running around and jumping up and down and thinking world domination. I was not going to go down that road again. I just quietly put it to one side and told no one.

I spent the next week refining my idea and worked out how to transport it. I would use a trailer. Yes, something low tech, simple, effective, and commonplace. I had to create something that people understood. If I could easily transport it, then somehow turn it into a building when it was deployed, that would be the key. I had now moved from my sketchpad to a software called Google Sketchup. It was an easy-to-use software that allowed you to create 3D designs in a very simple way. I taught myself how to use it and started to design in three dimensions. I was used to designing buildings so all my skills in this area came into play. I was excited by this new concept.

After two months, I showed it to Sarah, but she did not get it at all, "Why would anyone be interested in that?" She was my greatest critic, but I respected her point of view. I carried on. I had not shown it to my father; we were both very bruised from the loss in the building companies, and the timing did not feel right. I just kept going on my own.

About a month later I told Sarah, "Listen, I know you don't like this idea of my mine, and you have to endure a lot of my entrepreneurial ideas. But I really think you should hear me out one more time." She reluctantly agreed. What a trooper my dear Sarah is. She said to me recently that I enjoy spending more time with my computer than I do with her. I was taken aback by this comment and was quite hurt by it. I don't feel that way, but from her perspective, I can understand why she said that. Once I get into something—it's almost obsessive, compulsive. I am sorry, Sarah, for all those hours and days I could have spent with you. I believed I was doing it for us all, to make a better life for us through my passion for creation.

Our conversation ensued and I explained to her that this idea was no longer about my green building system but a showroom on wheels, a sales office, a store, a medical center, a sports outlet, and much more. It was a business on wheels, any business.

She then said something that was going change our lives and my career once again. "So you mean it's like a business in a box, a BIZBOX"

Fucking hell! She had done it again. She had given me the name to my new product and what would be come my new business. I was so excited.

That simple idea started to take on a life of its own. I registered the name with the United States Patent and Trademark Office with my sketch designs. I had been through this process before with EasiPour and now it was starting to make sense why I had travelled that arduous road. I had not yet shown it to my father, but one day he was in my office, and we were reviewing my accounts for the building company. It was not his business, but he always had an interest in what I was doing and I obliged. I decided to show him what I had created over the past six months or so. He was blown away and said it was the best idea he had seen me come up with. He always thought EasiPour was a winner that should have been a huge success. He still to this day does not know why it never really took off the ground.

"I love it," he said, "let's build one." I was completely shocked by this comment. My father is a bit like me. He loves a project and when he sees something he likes, he gets right on it. I assume that is where I caught the entrepreneurial bug. I was never taught to be afraid of failure. "Just try it," he would say. "If nothing else, you will learn from it."

My initial reaction was actually no. He seemed disappointed, and we just moved on with our meeting. About a week later, he called me and said that we should build one and that he was willing to help me with the initial cost. I could not believe it my father was once again willing to help me. I am so grateful to him for his encouragement all these years, and I am so lucky to have him in my life. There have been many times in my life when I thought I had lost him to ill health. It's amazing how different my life would have been without him. I am not exaggerating on two occasions he had a close call with death. Once when I was eighteen years old and working for the Kitchen company and once about ten years ago. Both times I thought I had lost him. He pulled through each time, but not without a long fight. My father is pure grit.

I eventually agreed to building one, and I set about finding a trailer company to build my BizBox.

Chapter 26: Two Canadians And A Brit

"**H**old still, Charles. Breathe in and breathe out" Dr. Gordon says to me as I feel the blood pressure monitor pump against my arm. Here we go again, I think to myself. I drift off and think about another doctor that's prevalent in my life.

Dr. Greg Sanders and I had become close friends since I had built his addition in 2007, and I knew that I could confide in him. I also knew he was very handy with computers and IT solutions. Greg had already built my website for my custom home building company, and I knew he would be perfect for BizBox. Even though he is a brilliant, Harvard graduate, and cardiologist by day; he is a computer whiz at night.

"Greg, it's Charles, how are you doing?" I asked.

"Great what's up?" he replied.

"Do you have five minutes I want to show you something?"

By now I had a virtual video of a 3D model of the BizBox that opened and closed. I had employed someone to make a little movie for me that showed how it opened up from a trailer and turned into a showroom. It was basic but very effective.

"Sure, how about Starbucks tomorrow at 9.00AM?" I agreed.

Our meeting was set, and I was excited to see his reaction to my new creation. There would be no reason for him to like it or pretend to like it. This would be a good place to start.

It was 9:00 AM, and Greg turned up. He was on the way to his office and more than likely had a day full of patients ahead of him. "So what have you got to show me, I'm intrigued," he began. I opened my laptop, said nothing, and just played the one-minute video. I just watched his face. He started smiling, looking back and forth between me and the computer. "Oh my god, Charles, this is fucking insane!" he exclaimed. He had so many questions and I had all the answers. He kept saying it "This is fucking insane!" over and over again. I was now laughing and knew I had something.

I asked him if he would be interested in being my IT guy and creating the website for the product and company for as long as we were in business, and in return, I would gift him some stock. He agreed and within a week, we had inked our deal. Soon after, Greg started to create version 1.0 of our website. We really had nothing, but it was a start. Once again, Greg believed in me and I was so grateful to him for that.

About a year earlier, I met Rick. He was also from Canada, like Greg. We met on Coronado Island in the summer during a family vacation from the Phoenix heat. My son and his daughter had become friends, and it was through them that Sarah and I began our friendship with Rick and his wife, Liz.

They had the same morals we did and understood that hard work and a good sense of direction were the framework of life. Rick and I hit it off from the start. He had grown his previous business in the franchise world and had really achieved the American dream. He had come to America many years ago as young man with an idea for a business, which had grown substantially.

Not long after I had inked my deal with Greg, I decided to call Rick and tell him about my interesting idea for his advice. I knew he had been in franchising, and I really thought that BizBox would be a great fit for that industry.

"Hey Rick, it's Charles. How's life treating you?" I started. Rick was essentially retired, following his sell-out some years earlier, I thought that he would have time to see my idea and give me some advice. "I have an idea for something, and I think it will fit well with the franchising world" I continued. "I could do with some advice on it. Do you have time to see me?"

"Sure, let's visit about it," he replied. That was about it. A few days later, we met. It was pretty much the same routine I had with Greg. I just played the video, sat back, and waited.

"Charles, this is very interesting," he said, "I really like it." We spent the next few hours discussing the product, its benefits, and possible uses. He agreed that it would be a good fit for the franchising world with many other business applications. He liked it so much that he offered to be an equal partner, but wanted to discuss it with his wife first. I was not expecting that at all. I patiently waited to hear his response.

You have to remember that Rick was pretty much retired and had climbed a huge mountain range in his previous business and reached the top. Even though he was only seven years older than me, he had succeeded and was not sure he wanted to start a new business all over again. On the other hand, he told me he was a little bored and yearned for something new to explore. He had looked at lot of deals and businesses over the past few years, but none of them excited him like the prospect of BizBox.

About a week later, I got a phone call. "Charles, it's Rick. I have done a lot of thinking, but I am sorry. I am going to pass. I am not sure I want to climb that mountain again." I completely understood and said,

"No problem, Rick, I really appreciate your help and let's stay in touch." He agreed, and I continued to row my own boat.

I continued to chart my own course and was invigorated by the future again. I was now doing two jobs. By day, I was continuing to build houses and remodels for my clients and by night, I was designing, refining, and developing BizBox. A few weeks after my call with Rick, I found a trailer builder in Phoenix to build my first BizBox. The company had been building trailers for a long time and seemed to have a lot of experience. We set about engineering the design I had worked on for many months and the owner of the company was excited by it. Within twelve weeks, I had my first BizBox. It was stunning and it turned from a trailer to a store in no more than twenty minutes. It actually looked almost exactly like my initial drawing I had created only nine months earlier. I was ecstatic, and I was ready to launch this brand new concept to the world.

My strategy was to create a very sophisticated video that showed how the BizBox would transform from a utility trailer to state-of-the art showroom or retail store. I was tight on money, so I had to find someone who would be willing to help put it together on a shoe-string budget. I had $5,000 for the budget, which was it. Sarah and I wrote and directed the script for the video. We engaged the studio ourselves and hired a great guy to do the filming. We found a friend of a friend to be the model.

We shot the video in one day and spent the next week editing. It turned out perfectly. In under two minutes, the whole production explained what BizBox was all about, how unique it was, and how easy it was to set up.

We finished the video just before July 1st, 2011 and I gave it to Greg to load up to our new website. He totally flipped out when he saw it. The timing was perfect as I was leaving for our summer vacation to Coronado Island. Just before I left, I decided to send Rick a link to the new website and the video.

The next morning I woke up to a voice message on my cell phone. It was Rick. "Charles, got your video. Give me a call...you rat!" he said laughing. This was the first time I had connected with Rick since I saw him a few months earlier. I don't think he could quite believe in that short space of time that I had actually built a fully working prototype, produced a website, and a superb marketing video. I think that is what tipped him over.

I called him back. "Hi Rick, how's it going?" I said cheekily.

"Well, Chuck, this is fantastic, and I have decided I want in!" he told me excitedly. To be honest, I was a little shocked by his reaction because I knew the last time we talked, he was happy being retired.

"Let me think about it." I responded,

"You actually want to think about me being your partner!" he continued, "Charles, recognize when you have a good thing staring you straight in the face!" This is what I liked about Rick—no bullshit and straight to the point. I agreed and he flew out to Coronado Island a few days later to put the deal together.

It was July 7th, 2011. This was the day we agreed our deal while sitting in the garden at The Glorietta Bay Hotel. We agreed on a price for the equal partnership and we spent the next few days strategizing on how to go about making my idea a real business.

Chapter 27: Where The Rubber Meets The Road

The blood pressure monitor continues to bring me in and out of consciousness, and I'm thinking, "Wow! This drug they have given me is amazing. I feel so relaxed and calm; I guess they could cut my head off and I wouldn't care."

"Hold still again, Charles," Dr. Gordon says confidently, "We're nearly done, and you're doing great. You're nearly at the end of the road."

Once again, I drift off into woozy heaven and think about another road.

A few months have now passed since our deal, and we had moved into our new headquarters in Scottsdale, Arizona, and Rick had brought all his expertise to get things moving. We quickly defined our roles in the company. As CEO, Rick was in charge of strategy, sales, growth and future capital investment. As President and Founder, I was in control of overall design, brand vision, marketing, patents, and development of new products. I had already designed a couple of new designs for the product, but we focused on the BizBox I had recently created.

Rick was energized, and he would come to Phoenix every few weeks where we would work extremely hard to grow interest in the product in order to develop some sales. At the time, I was back to wearing my rose colored glasses. Nothing could stop us and we were on a mission to bring BizBox to the world.

We attracted quite a lot of PR and were featured in newspapers and magazines, which certainly got the ball rolling. In the first month of opening our showroom, we had a number of companies come and look over our shiny new pop up store. During this time, Rick decided it would be a good idea to take the BizBox to a trade show. It was a franchising show, and he thought it would be good to show it off and gauge some feedback. The only problem was that it was in Toronto, Canada! I'm not sure if he just wanted to go back to his mother country or was looking for the furthest place on the map to road test the product. In any event, I remember saying to him that this was a long way to go for a show. Rick looked at me and said, "Charles, there are many people that let things get in the way of themselves, and they never achieve what they want. We have to push ourselves through that!" He was right, of course. Rick was very good at pushing us out of our comfort zone and still is. Yes, it would have been easier to go somewhere more local, but this journey actually proved a lot of things about both the team and the product.

The journey to and from Canada was arduous, but it was a very successful trip. We ended up learning that the BizBox could travel over five thousand miles with very little issue.

"All sound and fury amounting to nothing." People tend to tell you what you want to hear in business, and we were no exception. After doing a number of trade shows, we realized that this was not a good use of our time and money. We needed to get down to the nitty gritty details of building this company from the ground up. We targeted as many companies as we could, cold calling, sending out flyers, and anything else we could think of that would help drum up a sale.

Rick and I had invested our reputations in BizBox, and we had to stop drinking our own Kool Aid (as they say in the U.S.A.) and get real. It was now getting close to the end of 2011, and we had no sales or really any bites.

One day, Sarah and I were in the office and the phone rang. It was the marketing director of Skullcandy, the urban headphone brand. I knew a little about them as my boys had recently bought their products. The marketer had heard about our product from a business relationship we had with our graphic vehicle wrap company. The call went well, and they seemed to love the product and had been looking for a trailer like ours yet hadn't seen anything as cool or as creative as BizBox. A few days later, they flew to Phoenix and checked out the product. They loved it and wanted to rent it from us for about twelve months or so. I could not believe it. This was such welcome news as both Rick and I were becoming a bit twitchy.

I expected once again for things to happen fairly quickly, but it took about two months to agree to the deal and then about another three months to get their product built and delivered. We were starting to realize that things were not going to move quickly, and we were going to have to have nerves of steel and patience of a saint. During this time, we also agreed a loan deal with Barrett Jackson so they could use it for promotion at their largest classic car auction in Scottsdale.

The Skullcandy BizBox was a success, and they remain a client today. We saw a few deals trickle in, and it was tough to keep our spirits up. We started to attract AAA brands like The Phoenix Suns, Cricket Wireless, and Skullcandy. This gave us hope that we were on the right track.

Unfortunately, the economy was still in the gutter and money was very hard to come by, and we had really just started this business with great optimism and determination at an economic time that was the worst in history since the Great Depression. We powered on.

For almost a year now, we had been targeting lots of different businesses directly, ranging from golf companies to auto companies, healthcare and more. We sent out numerous low budget marketing campaigns and had little to show for it. It was depressing. Then, I got a call from Rick, and he said

"Charles, we're looking at this all wrong. No one cares who BizBox is because we are such small fish. We need to target the top marketing agencies in America and let them know about our products and its benefits. They need solutions for their clients and always want something new to show their clients." It was genius. He figured out that by going through the marketing agencies and providing them a solution to make them look like the hero to their client was a brilliant strategy. All we needed to do was to create a marketing campaign that would get us noticed by all the agencies. This was quite involved and it took some months as we created a multiple impression marketing campaign. I created all the graphics and flyers and Rick worked on the mailings. It took a while to trickle down, but we were soon getting inquiries and the phone was beginning to ring. In addition to this campaign, we felt it was time to develop the BizBox 2.0 that I had designed about a year earlier. The timing was perfect. We had listened to the feedback from events and customers that really wanted something that was visually appealing from the side on. The 2.0 did all that and much more.

We had our builder create a 2.0 prototype and decided to take it on the road for a tour of southern California and had appointments set up with numerous brands and agencies. We had employed a new member of staff some months earlier to help with transport and day-to-day work, and the three of us set off on our tour. It was hard work but exhilarating at the same time. The three of us rolled up our sleeves and got stuck in and, we must have set up the BizBox over twenty times during that trip. It paid off because we soon had new business and realized that seeing is believing. Not only that, my original idea of bringing the box to someone's location was key. All they had to do was walk out of their office and see the BizBox set up. It took up very little of their day and once they saw it, usually they were hooked.

We continued this campaign for many months, on a really small budget. Rick and I have always had the same opinion: value matters. Don't spend money where it's not necessary. Lots of large corporations waste so much money on new ideas and complicated initiatives. Our ethos was to always keep the business simple and effective.

By the end of 2012, we had attracted a new investor who took up some stock in the company, but business was still slow. Rick and I had earned almost nothing from the company. I was really beginning to feel the pinch. Both of us had worked our fingers to the bone and the prospect was still not too good. It just seemed like every time we got close to a deal, it fell away. This seemed to happen time and time again. I was close to a breaking point and actually told Rick that I would have to get a job to try and supplement my loss of income. He understood. It was now early January 2013, and we still did not have too much going on. I started to look for work, and it was not easy. I was at rock bottom. For the first time in life, I was writing my resume. The last time I had worked for someone else, I was seventeen years old. I was now forty-three, and my vision was not the best. It was indeed a very humbling time. Sarah was very stressed and was worried about our future. I was offered a job working for a friend of mine, which was actually a great position as president of a new division for his tech company. The pay wasn't great, but he knew that I was still trying to get BizBox off the ground and I was willing to take on the role and do what I could. It was a time of "needs must" and these are the things that test you to the limit.

About a week later, I got a phone call from my friend at the tech company, and I was told that he had decided to put the new division on hold due to the economy. He was sorry that the job was no longer available, but explained that he would get back to me in ninety days to discuss further. I remember putting down that phone and feeling like a complete failure. It was brutal. I went home that night feeling terrible. I was at a loss of what to do. I had no other job offers and BizBox was stumbling along.

I am not sure what came over me that night, but I do recall waking up in the night and thinking to myself, "No, I'm not giving this up. I'm not quitting, no fucking way!"

I called Rick first thing in the morning to tell him I was not quitting, and I would just keep going. Rick was actually on a fishing trip as he had gone away to clear his head. We were both licking our wounds.

"Rick, it's Charles. I'm not giving this up, we have worked too hard to give it up. Let's just keep going!" Rick and I have talked about this phone call on a number of occasions, and we both agree that this was a significant turning point in our business. It was pure grit and determination that was a testament to our nature. As I literally put the phone down with Rick, the phone rang again. This time, it was Oakley, who said they wanted a BizBox to rent. One day later, Mophie called and bought a BizBox. The day after that, a marketing agency we had been dealing with called and we sold two more for a world renowned brand. It was unbelievable! It was like a complete turn around, 360 degrees. I'm not sure if it was just timing, luck, staying power, or god playing his part in our story. Within one week, we had grossed more than what we had done the whole year before.

Chapter 28: Manufacturing!

It was now March, and we had orders coming in and our manufacturer was beginning to worry me. On the surface, it seemed like they were doing okay, but I could sense something wasn't right. We had placed a few orders with them-one was the two units for the world-renowned brand and we had paid the manufacturers their deposits. I would go and visit them from time to time as they were based about thirty minutes from our offices. I got to know the workmen and had a good relationship with them but started to hear rumors that they had not been paid for the last couple of paychecks. That was big red flag, and I approached the owner of the company and asked if everything was okay. He assured me that everything was great, but I did not quite believe him. I did a bit more digging and found out that the staff was not too happy and believed that he was in over his head. I couldn't believe it. We had just got this going and our manufacturer looked like he was in trouble.

Here we go again. We thought we had everything right and then bang! We get hit by a train. I quickly realized that he had taken our deposits and robbed Peter to pay Paul and we were Peter. It was time for a plan of action to get us out of a mess that was about to come crashing in. It was clear that the manufacturer had no money and we had to order all our materials to get our first box completed for the renowned brand while at the same time keep their men motivated to finish our product. It soon became very obvious that our business was in major trouble. If we had no builder, we had no business. We were faced with a tough decision. Do we go out of business knowing we had orders or do we take a huge leap and start our own manufacturing company?

We had come so far and looked over the precipice and stared defeat in the face only a few months earlier. We were not prepared to let someone else's mismanagement and poor business skills take our business down.

We drew up an action plan to start our own manufacturing business. Neither Rick or I wanted that, and it was never in our master plan to have a manufacturing arm of BizBox. It was going to be brutal, but we bit the bullet and went for it.

I spoke with a few of the men at the failing manufacturing company and asked if they would like to come and work for us. They all seemed very happy to do that as they had not been paid for sometime. They had all the experience necessary to build our products, but we had no clue of what to buy or what materials and tools we would need. Over the last year or so, I had watched fairly carefully at how the units were constructed but never really knew exactly how to build them. Over the next couple of weeks, while they were finishing the renowned brand BizBox at the failing company, I collated a list of materials and tools, and we started to purchase them and bring them to our showroom. We decided we would start our manufacturing facility in our existing showroom. We just had enough space to build one BizBox at a time in the showroom and room for the machinery and tools. We set up racks for the steel and placed all the machines in the space in one week. It was complete mayhem. We brought in another employee to help manage the workload and now there were four of us.

We were on a tight deadline to finish the Box and worked a twenty-four hour shift to get it completed. As soon as it was done, we transported it to our new manufacturing facility. Fortunately, we still had to pay the manufacturing company a final payment for the completed unit, and this gave us some leverage when it came time to resolve how much money they had stolen from us.

It was probably the most stressful business time of my life. We had set up a new facility in our showroom and six new employees were due to start with us. We did not know if they would turn up, and we had expended all this money. It was a complete leap of faith.

Monday arrived, and the guys turned up right on time. We were up and running. Of course, all the guys' phones were ringing all week as the old company wanted to know where they were. It was not long before they realized they had jumped a sinking ship. I then spent the next few weeks ordering materials and keeping the guys going, which was completely exhausting. It was like going back to my old days of building when I first started out. I was learning quickly on the job. I immersed myself in the construction of the product. I really needed to learn every aspect of trailer building. Everyday I would get up early, and it felt like I was giving myself an injection of stress right into my veins. I had never worked so hard or been so tired in my life. I was close to breaking point, and Rick knew it.

My brain was mush, and my focus was wavering. I just kept going and pushed through it. We delivered the second unit on time, which was a complete miracle and we had now built "our" first BizBox. It was clear we could not build more than one at a time in the showroom, so we decided to find a larger manufacturing space. About one week later, we found a new space in Phoenix, close to the airport and then proceeded to move everything over there. Again, it was complete chaos and within one week, we were up and running in our new space. We could build at least four at a time in that space and we set up a dedicated bay for welding, and then the unit would move through the stages on a type of production line. We created our own inventory store that was all numbered and created racks and areas for different tasks. I took all my skills from building and applied the same logic. Rick brought all his skills of systems and operating procedures and within one month, we had a slick manufacturing operation. We now had twelve employees, and our overhead was huge. We had gone from a sales and marketing business to a manufacturing business overnight.

Managing the men was not too easy and additional employees increase problems. Rick and I were worried that we needed to keep up the orders; otherwise, we would be out of business pretty quickly due to our overhead. The orders did come in from more prestigious brands. At the same time, we decided to take our profits and build an inventory so we had units to sell or rent. That was particularly hard because neither of us earned any money. It all went back in the business.

Chapter 29: Health!

Summer soon came around, and I was completely out of steam and looking forward to my break in Coronado. Rick was also going this summer, and we agreed that we would take some time to relax and reflect on the craziness, but work each day. About two weeks before heading to California, I woke up one night and vomited in my sleep. I felt awful and did not know what was going on. For many years, I had suffered with stomach problems and had pain. I put it down to stress and worry. As I was recovering the next day, I was watching a TV show about people with gallbladder problems. As they discussed their issues, I could not believe it, they were describing exactly my symptoms.

One week later, I ended up having my diseased gallbladder removed. After all these years of suffering, it was my gallbladder. The surgery was not too bad, but the recovery was pretty rough. I was already pretty much exhausted, but this just took me down to a whole other level. I tried to go back to work for a bit, but it was hard, and I was now really looking forward to my break in the California sun.

July 1st came around, and we headed to Coronado as we always did. I left our new manufacturing facility in the hands of our staff and kept in contact with them on a daily basis. I was still very weak from my recent surgery, and I was walking gingerly. One week later,

I was due to go on a business trip with Rick to see a client in southern California. I was just brushing my teeth, and my right eye started to go crazy and was flickering. I knew instantly something was wrong. I called Rick who was actually waiting outside my apartment to pick me up, and I said "Rick, I can't go. I am sorry! I have to go to an eye doctor right away. My right eye is going nuts!" He was confused and concerned at the same time. This had come out of nowhere.

I remembered I had seen a retinal surgeon in California one summer some years before about my left eye because I was having problems with it. I found the same company online and called them. I headed over there with Sarah, and the outlook did not look good. They told me the vitreous was detaching from the eye, and that it could be pulling at my retina. They told me not to worry but keep a close check on it and to come back if I had more symptoms. One week later, I found myself in that retinal surgeons chair hearing the bad news that my eye had detached, and I needed immediate surgery to save my sight.

You know the rest.

By the end of 2013, we had steadily grown the business and had developed three new products to go with our already existing ones. We had scraped and scraped our way through the ups and downs on a number of occasions but we prevailed. It was immensely tough for the both of us with my serious health issues and business complications.

During a very dark time for me, a bright light appeared out of the blue that would then change the course of our company once again. In early October of that year, we received some incredible news. We had been awarded a twenty-year utility patent from the United States Patent Office. It was such a welcome relief to all the hard work we had endured. The patent application that I had applied for some years earlier had become a reality. It was official; I was now an inventor. All those years I had chased that dream, and now it was a reality. I had truly created something unique and of significant value.

Rick and I agreed that we should license our patents and out-source the production of our products and go back to being a company of innovation, sales, and marketing. Manufacturing had been an essential part of our growth and learning, but it was now time to reduce our overhead and go lean. We decided to close the manufacturing facility and embark on this new bold business plan. A few months later, we had signed our first license deal and have since grown the company and exposure for our products exponentially. We have completed work for many more AAA brands and publicly traded companies. The story of BizBox is far from over, and the future looks bright.

Winners never quit, quitters never win.

Chapter 30: Back To Earth

The surgery was over, and I went through the usual process of head down for a week while listening to audio books on my iPhone and trying to get my life into a normal routine. It was incredibly tough for both my family and me for many months. I was legally blind and could not drive, work, or do too much at all. For the first time in my in my life, I was forced to examine where I had come from and where I was going. I did not know my future. All I had was the present. You often hear that when someone goes through a trauma, whether it be a situation like mine or a tragic death, a person is told to take life one a day at a time. It's so true. All you can do is take life one day at a time. You can't think further than that. I still had a business to run and employees and a manufacturing facility. It could not have been much worse. I had so much pressure on me, and I could only really carry on and try to appreciate what I had.

There were many down days, and I had to really muster all my inner strength to stay positive and strong for my family. Sarah would find me using a magnifying glass to try and read emails on my computer. I know that was heartbreaking for her, but all I was doing was surviving. It's truly amazing how the body adapts to a situation. I did feel quite lonely though. I felt as if I were in a world that went on without me. I could not watch the television or go to a movie. All the things I once enjoyed were gone.

I went to the gym as often as I could to do a light workout to try and stay fit, but I was self conscious of my dark glasses and eye patch. I became angry and confused and started to retract, while trying to keep a public face of strength and calm. I spent many days, when I would just sit at my desk and I would cry really hard. It felt actually good to let out that emotion and once I was done I just moved forward.

The days and weeks went by very slowly, and I tried to stay focused on the bigger picture in life. Rick and I would talk about work each day, which actually gave me a sense of normality, and I at least felt like I could still contribute. Sarah and my boys were amazing, and they made me laugh although I know it must have been brutal to watch me go through my struggles. That hurt me a lot. I felt bad for them more than myself.

As time went on, I adjusted to the fact that this might be my life and I was okay with that. It wasn't too bad; I could see a bit out of my left eye, which allowed me to get around on my own and be slightly functional. I just missed the detail. It was the detail that killed me. Detail had been everything in my life, whether it was designing a kitchen, a building, a new product. I needed to see the detail. It was the very core of my being. I could not focus on anything, everything was just blurry. I went to see a movie and even though the screen was huge, it was blurry. I tried to enjoy it, but it was just no good.

I was prepared to accept my new life, and I was going to make the best of it whatever the outcome may be. I tried to continue to design products even though I had to squint and make my computer screen enormous. I coped. I was just treading water.

Well you only need the light when its burning low,
Only miss the sun when it starts to snow,
Only know you love her when you let her go,
Only know you've been high when you're feeling low,

Only hate the road when you're missin' home,
Only know you love her when you let her go,

by Passenger

It's indeed amazing how we miss something when it's no longer there and when we have it we don't really appreciate it. I had gone though this for a reason, the past six years and six eye surgeries, I could not believe it was just *because.*

We have to genuinely take time and appreciate what we have. Try to be present, try to be real. try to be kind, try to always be positive. I decided as soon as I went in for the operation, I was not going to be a victim and moan about my problem. Yes, I was scared and I had every right to be but I was going to be positive and instill positivity in my life. I was going to do whatever it took to make my life the best I could.

This was a scary time, and I was actually grateful that I went through it. I know that sounds strange, but that is how I feel. I was grateful to realize what it's like to have something taken away that we take for granted from the day we are born. It's the first thing we do- see, smell, touch, hear. Lose one of those senses and it changes your perspective.

It is almost exactly a year as I write this to what was a pivotal moment in my life.

It was Rosh Hashanah, and I had been through hell and back and on the eve of Rosh Hashanah (a holy day in itself) I said to myself that I will rise again and start my year all over again tomorrow. I wanted to put behind me all my troubles and focus on a fresh start. That day, I was hoping to see my son play soccer, and I had asked a friend to lend me their binoculars so I could try and zoom in and see him. They kindly obliged. Prior to the game I picked them up and I looked through them. I was in my kitchen

167

and I zoomed in on the trees outside. It was unreal, I could see out of my right eye!

I could not believe it! My brain was not even registering what had just happened. I was doubting myself. I could see the leaves clearly and in DETAIL! It was completely unbelievable. I then started looking at everything, and my eye was working. For many months, I had not been able to see much further than a few feet.

I called Dr. Gordon and told him what had happened, and I asked him if I could go and get some glasses to help with the vision. I was a long way off from having good sight, but right then and there, I knew he had repaired my retina. I was finally SAFE, SAFE, SAFE.

The next day was Rosh Hashanah, and I went to synagogue as I always do where I was just so thankful for my life and my journey. A week later it was Yom Kippur a day when we atone for all our sins. It is a day of fasting and reflection on your life. This was the perfect backdrop to my own reflection. I spent the whole time in synagogue in quiet prayer and reflection. Right at the end of the service, after nearly twenty four hours of fasting and internal reflection, is when the "gates of heaven" close and we all start fresh for a new cleansed beginning.

Something my dear friend and Rabbi said to the congregation during that moment was so pivotal to me. He said,

"We can all send our souls up to heaven when the gates of heaven are open at this sacred time, but it's when the gates close and we have to return to earth it's how we return that matters. How will we go forward with our lives when we return to earth?"

It was so profound, and I felt tears streaming down my face. I can remember hugging my Tallit close to my heart and feeling an immense energy running through me. I would come back down to earth and see my life in a completely different way. I would go forward and take whatever positive action I could. It was time to leave behind the old year that was full of trials and obstacles and replace them with only goodness and clarity of thought. I would encourage and help others to be better, and I would work harder each day to be more present and more alert to my surroundings, looking at my life through a new lens. I would try to be calmer and more considered in my approach to everything. I so much appreciated the leaves on the trees, the sunset and sunrise, my children's faces and smiles, my wife's gentle touch, her beautiful blue eyes, and strawberry blonde hair. I appreciated the beauty of my surroundings and the joy of watching a movie once again. As soon as I could drive again, I appreciated sitting in traffic and watching the world go by. I was again a part of the world, a part of the nature of human doings. Although this time, I was not just running around aimlessly getting caught up in the noise of our world and letting each day go by like I had used to without really noticing it. I was waking up each day with a sense of gratefulness and joy for a new day, even if it was a Monday. I had become a human being again and was enjoying just *being*.

I had once again reached a crossroads in my life, and I had chosen a new path.

Chapter 31: Discovering True Vision

Writing this book in itself has been an enlightening journey. I did not know what to expect from writing it or where it would take me. Like most things in my life, I just visualized it finished, sitting on my desk. I could see what the cover looked like, and at that point I knew I had to write it. I just started to write one day and the words flowed out. I had no plan or framework for it. I knew I had to get from point A to point B like most things in my life.

However, along the way, I discovered myself writing something completely unexpected. Beginning to write this book, I thought that finding my true vision was going to be about my struggles and how I overcame them each time. I was wrong.

As the words flowed out and they became a reality on my computer I discovered a pattern, a pattern or a continuos thread that occurred throughout my life that was one of encouragement and advocacy. One Sunday morning, over coffee with my good friend Greg Sanders, I was discussing this pattern with him and it was something he said that was a light bulb moment. "Charles, it's the words of encouragement along the way that have made you!" he continued, "You showed passion, People saw something in you, and you were not afraid to try, and the people around you were attracted to it." He was right.

From the age of seven when Mr. Mckay believed in me and gave me a voice, he gave me encouragement. My parents encouraging me and believing in me, my teachers and Housemaster Dr. Hershon, my first internships and work experience in those drawing offices to my beautiful wife allowing me to follow my dreams and my business partners investing in my vision and jumping on board-it's the collaboration of people and how we interact with each other that makes us better people. How we treat each other and how we respect each other and how we encourage each other—that makes the difference.

I realized what Greg was talking about; it was my passion that attracted others, whether it was wanting to wear long trousers at school or my passion for art or my ideas for a new business. It was that passion that allowed me to encourage and engage with others to join in on my path.

Once again, my wise friend Pinchas said something recently that struck a cord with me, "A piece of coal burning on its own will burn for a while, but will eventually burn out. You need other pieces of coal to help it continue to burn." I thought about this for a while and realized that this is very apt to my life. I feel that my passion is like that piece of coal burning, but it was the advocates and collaborations in my life that helped fuel my aspirations and goals and kept them glowing. We all need people around us to help our internal fires to continue to shine and grow. If we think we can do it alone, without encouragement and help, then we are foolish. Think for a moment of how different our world would be if we all encouraged and helped each other more often. Think about what those words of *encouragement* do for us when they come at a pivotal time from someone we respect such as a teacher, a Headmaster, a spouse, a father, a mother, a brother, a grandparent, a friend or a business partner. When we hear those words we soar, and we are better human *beings*. We achieve greater things, and we all appreciate and value our lives so much more.

Our vision *is* truly different if we have had advocates in our life and encouragement along the way. I am positive that the way I view the world is different from someone who has not had encouragement or people that believed in them. I have to believe that someone who only receives criticism is less likely to view the world in a positive way because they have a different view of the world.

If we can all discover that we are better when we work together and inspire others with our encouraging words, then we can take that model and pass it on to our children. We can help them grow up with the knowledge that they can believe in themselves and be strong and courageous in their conviction. We can pass on that *burning coal* to them and let them know that they are not alone and that coal can burn brightly forever as *they* pass it on and so forth.

As you have read, I have had to climb over many obstacles in my life, which took determination, perseverance, and grit. But that's just a small part of my journey. Receiving encouragement, whether it was obvious or subliminal from people that I respected at pivotal times in my life, is what truly gave me the strength, courage, and the protection to jump higher and help me conquer those tough times. It was that belief in self that had been instilled in me throughout my life, through those encouraging words, collaborations, and *then* actions, that I was able to discover my *true vision*.

Made in the USA
Lexington, KY
18 February 2015